AARP®

Genealogy Online

tech to connect

AARP®

Genealogy Online

tech to connect

by Matthew L. Helm and April Leigh Helm

WILEY

John Wiley & Sons, Inc.

DISCARD 939. H

AARP® Genealogy Online: Tech to Connect

Published by
John Wiley & Sons, Inc.
111 River Street
Hoboken, NJ 07030-5774
www.wiley.com

WILEY

Connections That Work for You

Are you searching for your ancestral roots, but you don't know where to look? Or have you started to pull together your family history and gotten stuck on a particular detail? You've turned to the right place for help.

Dedicated to helping you strengthen your family ties and navigate the world of technology, AARP has joined with the *For Dummies* brand to offer the best advice and solutions for using *tech to connect*.

This step-by-step guide offers ways to

- Find free and low-cost software, websites, and other resources
- Use social networking sites to locate family members you didn't know you had
- Build your own site to compile and share information with relatives
- Create a family project that will delight all generations

Whatever your experience with genealogy — online or offline — our easy-to-follow resource helps you build your family tree.

Ready to start digging? Let's go!

AARP is a nonprofit, nonpartisan membership organization that helps people 50 and older improve their lives. For more than 50 years, AARP has been serving our members and society by creating positive social change. AARP's mission is to enhance the quality of life for all as we age; lead positive social change; and deliver value to members through information, service and advocacy.

About the Authors

Matthew L. Helm is the chief executive officer of Boneyard Creek Heritage, Inc., a family and local history services company. He is also the chief history officer at HistoryKat.com, Inc., a company that specializes in digitizing and posting historical records online. The creator and maintainer of the award-winning Helm's Genealogy Toolbox and the Helm/Helms Family Research Page (and a variety of other websites), Matthew speaks at national genealogical conventions and lectures to genealogical and historical societies. He holds a bachelor of arts degree in history and a master of science degree in library and information science from the University of Illinois at Urbana-Champaign. His full-time job is serving as the executive director of administrative technologies at Illinois State University.

April Leigh Helm, who is the president of HistoryKat.com, Inc., and Boneyard Creek Heritage, Inc., works as an enterprise systems coordination specialist for the University of Illinois. A lecturer on genealogy and other topics for various conferences and groups, April holds a bachelor of science degree in journalism and a master of education degree in higher education administration from the University of Illinois at Urbana-Champaign.

Together, the Helms have coauthored several books in addition to the six editions of *Genealogy Online For Dummies*, including *Family Tree Maker For Dummies, Your Official America Online Guide to Genealogy Online* (all published by John Wiley & Sons, Inc.), and *Get Your Degree Online*.

Dedication

For Kyleakin and Cambrian

Authors' Acknowledgments

We offer special thanks to our friends at John Wiley & Sons, who provided invaluable guidance and feedback on this book: Katie Mohr, Kim Darosett, Rebecca Whitney, Sharon Mealka, and Pat O'Brien.

Publisher's Acknowledgments

We're proud of this book; please send us your comments at http://dummies.custhelp.com. For other comments, please contact our Customer Care Department within the U.S. at 877-762-2974, outside the U.S. at 317-572-3993, or fax 317-572-4002.

Some of the people who helped bring this book to market include the following:

Acquisitions, Editorial, and Vertical Websites

Project Editor: Kim Darosett

Acquisitions Editor: Katie Mohr

Copy Editor: Rebecca Whitney

Technical Editor: Sharon Mealka

Editorial Assistant: Leslie Saxman

Sr. Editorial Assistant: Cherie Case

Cover Photos: ©amana images / Jupiter Images (main image); ©iStockphoto.com / Ivan Stevanovic (background image)

Composition Services

Project Coordinator: Kristie Rees

Layout and Graphics: Claudia Bell, Carrie A. Cesavice

Proofreader: BIM Indexing & Proofreading Services

Indexer: BIM Indexing & Proofreading Services

Publishing and Editorial for Technology Dummies

Richard Swadley, Vice President and Executive Group Publisher

Andy Cummings, Vice President and Publisher

Mary Bednarek, Executive Acquisitions Director

Mary C. Corder, Editorial Director

Publishing for Consumer Dummies

Kathleen Nebenhaus, Vice President and Executive Publisher

Composition Services

Debbie Stailey, Director of Composition Services

Table of Contents

Introduction

We authors like to think that we live in the golden age of family history. When we first began our personal research, the process was time- and travel-intensive. After visiting the National Archives (or one of its regional archives) to sign out a reader for studying microfilm, we would consult the archive's index books in the hope of finding a trace of elusive ancestors. When we were lucky, we would find a clue in an index, which enabled us to pull the correct microfilm from the long rows of cabinets. After shuffling to the reader, we would scroll, seemingly endlessly, to find the page number from the index.

Fortunately, over the past decade, family history research has taken a quantum leap forward. After the spotty transcription of key historical records on CD-ROM came the systematic digitization and indexing of census records, first on CD-ROM and later on the web. Now a new age has begun, as evidenced by the digital release of the 1940 United States census directly online rather than on microfilm, accompanied by the community effort to index this census in its entirety and to make the index available for free. Beyond traditional sources of family history research, science is advancing DNA techniques. First Y-DNA and mitochondrial DNA were used, and now refined techniques allow researchers to use autosomal DNA to fill in holes in their research. (That might sound complicated, but we'll show you that it's not.)

In addition to progress in the availability of census records, millions of military, vital (such as birth certificates and death records), tax, and land records are now digitized and indexed online. Though you still can't complete your entire family history exclusively from online sources, you can make a good start from the comfort of your own home.

About This Book

Though millions of records are now online, no single comprehensive way to find all of them exists. You need a strategy for locating and evaluating the evidence that you find online, and that's where this book comes in. We help you sort out where to begin your search and point you toward key sites. At the same time, we give you tips for using these sites effectively, to save you time and (we hope) frustration. And you can find easy ways to create a family tree and share that with the rest of your family.

Keep in mind that this book covers genealogical websites, software, and resources that are most commonly used and preferred at the time of this book's printing. We are not endorsing these sites and software over others, but in our experience and through extensive research, we have found these resources to be the most effective and useful for our own online genealogy.

Before you start following the step-by-step instructions in this book, you need to know a few basic research strategies that can save you time in the long run. If you're at the beginning of your family history journey, we suggest that you keep these steps in mind:

Plan: Always start with a plan. Begin by thinking about members of your family whom you know something about, and jot down particular information about them that you want to confirm. For example, start by trying to find records that can confirm vital information about a parent or grandparent, such as the dates of their births, marriages, and deaths. You can better focus your research by establishing specific goals.

Collect: Before booting up your computer and going online, collect whatever information you can from records around your house (such as birth, marriage, or death records, insurance documents, wills, and deeds) or from interviewing other family members. In this way, you can build a foundation for evaluating the information you find online to ensure that you're on the right track toward tracing your ancestors.

Research: After you establish this foundation, you can start researching. Online research, as covered in this book, is only one of many tools you should use to paint the complete picture of your family history. You can also use a combination of online and traditional resources, such as records from county clerks, libraries, cemeteries, and genealogical societies.

Consolidate: After a trip online or to a local repository, organize all the material you've gathered. Consolidating this information into genealogical database software is an ideal solution to provide not only a storage location for your findings but also a safety backup. Remember to cite the sources of your evidence in the database to assist you in confirming information later, such as when someone retraces your research.

Distill: The final step is to use your genealogical database to distill information for your next search. You can use the reporting features of the software to find gaps in your records or to uncover conflicting information, such as different birth dates for the same individual. You can also use the information in your database to share with other researchers, who can help you by sharing their research. Always respect the privacy of living individuals, and respect copyright laws when sharing information.

 Keep in mind that you can't believe *everything* you find online, in books, or even in primary source records. You can't assume that certain information is factual simply because it's in print. We have found many mistakes in the research of others — even in published research. New record sets are released every day that can change the conclusions made in previous research. When our youngest daughter was born, the hospital attempted three times to complete her birth registration paperwork correctly. Had we accepted the original paperwork without checking it, our daughter's name would have been misspelled, the time of birth would have been off by 12 hours, and a parent's name would have been incorrect. The lesson: Validate every piece of information you find, and even verify primary records with other primary records to form a conclusion supported by evidence.

Who This Book Is For

If you're the kind of person who has an interest in family roots, who loves to solve puzzles, and who wants to use technology to discover a new wealth of resources, *AARP Genealogy Online: Tech to Connect* is definitely for you. Even if you don't consider yourself tech-savvy, this book can be your guide to your past.

If you haven't yet started researching your family history, you need to know that you're likely to become hooked on it. You'll always have another record to find, another person to connect with, or another resource to explore. Researching your family history can consume a lot of time, but it's well worth the effort.

Conventions

To make this book as easy to use as possible, we have used certain *conventions,* or standard ways of identifying key concepts within the book:

- Whenever we introduce a new concept, we *italicize* the word or phrase (as in the following bullet) so that you can easily find it when you need it.
- Whenever we refer to a website for the first time, we include its web address (or *URL*) so that you can type the location into your web browser and immediately start your research on that site. If you're reading an electronic version of this book, simply click the URL to pop over to the site.

■ When we want you to type something onscreen, we spell it out in **bold** type.

■ Whenever we introduce you to a web resource, we search as generically as possible so that you can find answers to your research questions no matter what they are.

■ When we have more to say than will fit into a single step, we use sidebars to enhance the list of steps or to provide you with more useful information.

■ The figures that we sprinkle generously throughout this book should be helpful for visual learners as well as for hands-on readers. The figures help you stay on the path at key junctures in the activities in the book.

How This Book Is Organized

Though you have many ways to research your family history, you need some basic experience before we turn you loose on the larger websites and more complex resources. Here's a rundown of the order in which topics are introduced in the book:

Get your feet wet by researching yourself (Chapter 1). Chapter 1 explains the research techniques to use when researching family members, whether they're members of your current family or ancestors from long ago. We walk you through the steps to write an autobiography and use records from your own life as evidence — the same kind of evidence you need in order to fill in the family history of your ancestors.

Create family trees and store your research (Chapters 2 and 3). Your research isn't helpful if you don't keep track of the evidence you find online and via other research methods. We tell you how to use genealogy database software to create a family tree online — two resources that can help you focus your research and fill in any gaps that you find.

Search the web (Chapter 4). Millions of pages on the web contain family history information, and you have to find the right one to meet your needs. We walk you through the steps to use web search engines efficiently, and we provide you with search strings that can focus your results.

Discover the wealth of information at the big-name research sites (Chapters 5 and 6). Successful family-history research on the web usually involves either Ancestry.com or FamilySearch.org — or both. These two sites contain millions of records between them and research guides that can teach you ways to discover even more records in repositories around the world.

Take advantage of free information on government sites (Chapter 7). One thing the government does well is generate evidence for family history researchers. We cover some helpful websites that feature government records, including military, land, and immigration.

Map your research (Chapters 8 and 9). Using geographical resources helps you put your ancestors' lives into context. You can discover your ancestors' living conditions and use geographical records to locate their hiding places (in records, that is). And, of course, you can use maps to visit the places where your ancestors lived.

Capitalize on smaller record sites (Chapters 10 and 11). A number of smaller sites specialize in a particular type of record set (or sets), such as military and local records. We describe how to use some of these sites and give you tips to discovering the unique resources of each one.

Communicate by using social networking sites (Chapter 12). Sites dedicated to genealogy and family history aren't the only places to discover hints about your ancestors. We introduce you to ways to use social networking sites, such as Facebook, to communicate with other researchers who can assist you with your research.

Explore DNA research (Chapter 13). DNA is truly the new frontier of genealogy research. Many tests are available these days, and we help you select one for the type of answers you're seeking.

Mobilize your research on a tablet or smart phone (Chapter 14). You can take your research with you almost anywhere you go. It's easily contained and accessed in a *tablet* — a compact and lightweight tool that uses applications (or *apps*) to maximize your research experience while you're in the field.

Chapter 1

Writing Your Autobiography with arcalife

You can begin the journey to find your family history in many different ways. We believe that the best way is to focus on the person you know best — yourself. By completing an autobiographical sketch, you learn some of the questions to ask about your ancestors and start getting acquainted with the types of records you use when researching others. And, who knows? You might even learn a little about yourself in the process. For a fun way to start, follow a guided autobiography online.

While there are several sites that allow you to enter biographical information as a way of producing a print publication, arcalife is the only site that we have found that asks you a set of interview questions, and your answers are then merged to form a family history. But rather than suggest that you create a complete family history with arcalife, we recommend that you start with your own autobiography so that you can become comfortable using online resources to help with your research.

tech 2 to connect

activities

- Creating a free arcalife registration
- Specifying the privacy settings
- Noting memories on the site
- Listing experiences
- Assembling your online autobiography

Creating a Free arcalife Registration

The first step in writing an autobiography on arcalife is to complete the free registration. You can sign up by using the site's 1-Step Free Signup option, as described in these steps:

1. Point your browser to www.arcalife.com.
2. In the rightmost column, find the area marked 1-Step Free Signup (see Figure 1-1).
3. Fill out your name, e-mail address, password, birthdate, and gender in the appropriate fields.
4. In the Enter Code box, type the code that appears to the right of the Enter Code field.
5. Read the terms of use and then select the Agree to Terms of Use box.
6. Click the Sign Up button to continue. The page redirects you to your personalized arcalife home page.

Figure 1-1

Controlling Privacy Settings

Before entering your personal information at the arcalife site, you must choose who can see the information you're placing there. An easy way to do this is to change the privacy settings on the site. Until you're more comfortable with how arcalife works, we suggest that you set the privacy settings to their highest settings. Keep in mind that you can always restore less restrictive settings later. Follow these steps to change your arcalife privacy settings:

1. Log in to the arcalife site. To do so, click the Login link in the upper-right corner of the home page. When the Login pop-over box appears, type the e-mail address and password you used while registering and click the Login button. (This *pop-over box* is similar to a dialog box except that it expects you to complete its fields and click a button to make it disappear.)

2. In the Tools and Settings section of the leftmost column on the page, click the Privacy Settings link. The Privacy Settings page appears, as shown in Figure 1-2. You can set the privacy settings for every area of the site.

3. To set the privacy settings for the Life Archives section, click the Change Settings button in the Life Archives box. The Privacy Settings pop-over box appears.

4. To choose the highest privacy level, click the Private radio button.

5. Click the Save button to save the settings.

6. Repeat Steps 3–5 to set the privacy settings for the remaining areas of the site.

Figure 1-2

Noting Memories on the Site

After you have set up an account on arcalife and set its security level, it's time to begin listing memories. Include your own memories and the memories that other people have of you. Follow these steps:

1. Log in to the arcalife website. (See Step 1 in the preceding section.)

2. From your personalized page, click the My Life tab at the top of the page. The tab is on the green arc that spans the top of the personalized page.

3. On the My Life page are a number of tabs on which you can provide information. Fill out the information on the Profile tab for yourself, and then click the Save button. Note that some of your information is already prepopulated, as a result of your site registration.

   The Profile tab has some fields that you don't need to worry about, such as Date of Death, Place of Death, and Final Resting. These fields are used in other areas of the site, if you later choose to use the site to enter information about your ancestors.

4. Click the Memories tab.

5. Click the New Memory link. The Write a New Memory dialog box appears.

6. Click an event in the Select a Life Chapter pane. For example, clicking My Birth populates the Select a Subject pane with questions, as shown in Figure 1-3. It also places the text *My Birth* in the topmost blank line in the bottom half of the Write a New Memory dialog box.

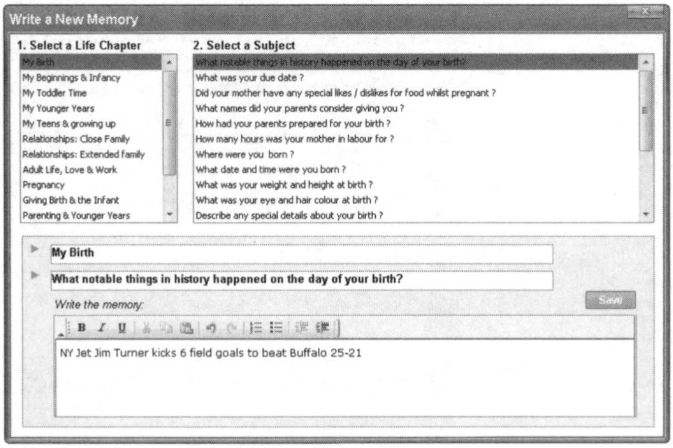

Figure 1-3

7. Click a question in the Select a Subject pane. The question you select is populated in the second blank box in the bottom half of the screen.

8. In the Write the Memory text box, answer the question you selected. You can add as many details as you want.

You can use the formatting tools at the top of the box to bold, italicize, underline, number, or bullet-point your text.

9. When you finish adding details, click the Save button. The screen moves back to the Memories page, and your memory is added, as shown in Figure 1-4. You can use the Edit Memory and Delete Memory links on the right side of the memory to make changes.

10. Repeat Steps 5–9 to add memories.

After you collect a lot of memories, you can use the Show All Memories filter drop-down list to reduce the displayed memories to a specific life chapter.

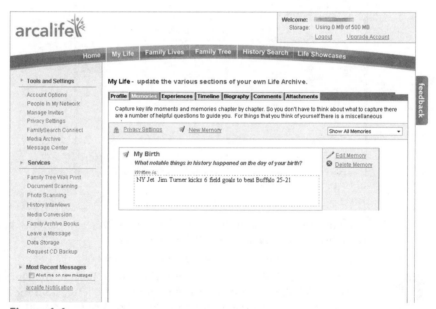

Figure 1-4

Listing Experiences

Another way to place information in your autobiography is to create experiences. *Experiences* are specific events that occurred on particular dates. Follow these steps to list an experience:

1. From the My Life page, click the Experiences tab. The default life event, Birth, is already displayed when you click it.

2. Click the View/Edit link to enter information about your birth. A new Experience dialog box appears onscreen, as shown in Figure 1-5.

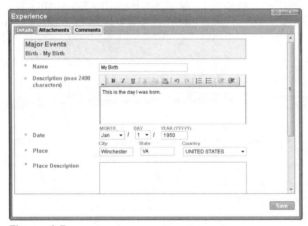

Figure 1-5

3. Type information about the experience in the Description field. Note that the field holds a maximum of 2,400 characters.

4. Type the city, state, and country in the Place fields.

The Country field is a drop-down list. If you were born in the United States, you can click the Country field and then press the letter *u* on the keyboard to quickly reach the area of the drop-down box where the United States appears.

5. Enter additional information in the Place Description field.

6. Add a tag word to make the experience easier to find. To do this, click the Add Tag link, enter the tag, and then click the Add button. The tag appears in the Tags box.

Tag words are simple descriptions you can use to locate items quickly. For example, you can add a tag, such as *Chicago,* for the location of the birth experience. Then you can search on the place name later to see all experiences that happened at that location.

7. Click the Attachments tab to upload a file related to your experience. For example, if you have a birth record, you can attach a copy of it to the experience. Be aware that attaching a record stores a copy of it on the arcalife servers. Please read the Terms of Use page on the site before doing this so that you understand how the site uses your documents.

8. Click the Comments tab to provide further details on your experience. If you have additional comments about it, you can type them in the field. When you're done, click the Leave Comment button.

9. Click the Save button after you have completed your experience. Your experience is added, as shown in Figure 1-6.

10. To add experiences, click the New Experience link, and repeat Steps 3–9 as appropriate.

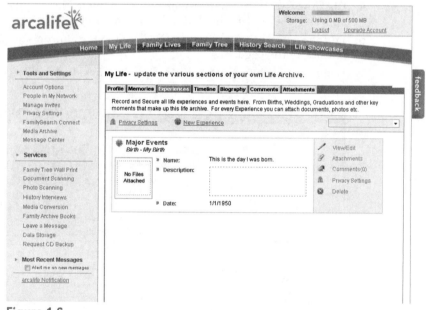

Figure 1-6

Assembling Your Online Autobiography

After adding all your memories and experiences to arcalife, you can see them consolidated into a single autobiography by using the Biography tab. Follow these steps:

1. From the My Life page, click the Create Biography link to assemble your autobiography. A new pop-over window appears, labeled Create New Biography.

2. Enter a name for your biography in the Please Provide a Title for This Biography field.

3. Select a border for the biography by clicking the appropriate radio button.

4. Click the Create button to assemble the completed biography. A new window appears, labeled Scrapbook Editor, as shown in Figure 1-7.

5. Edit the pages of your biography by selecting the appropriate page from the left side of the page.

6. When you finish formatting the biography, click the Save Book button.

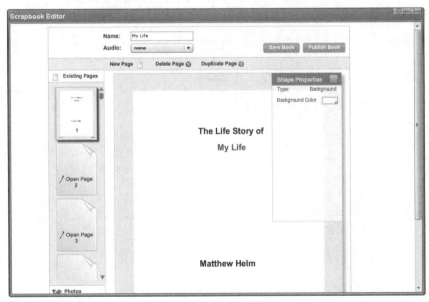

Figure 1-7

Chapter 2

Creating an Online Family Tree

There are a few sites that you can use to create an online family tree. For example, MyHeritage.com and Geni (www.geni.com) allow you to store your family history information online. The most full-featured site for creating an online family tree is Ancestry.com. You can not only see the information on their Web site, but also view it on the go with their iPad and iPhone app.

Ancestry.com is the largest online, for-profit, genealogical website — the site has several million records available. Some records are textual, and others include original, scanned images. A few records on the site are freely available; however, most require a paid membership. In this chapter, we cover one free service: building an online family tree. The online family tree can help you keep track of all your ancestors and share information with other researchers who, in turn, might be able help you.

tech connect to

activities

- Starting a new, online family tree
- Adding facts to a profile
- Citing sources
- Adding media
- Leaving comments for visitors
- Reviewing hints
- Connecting with other members

Starting a New, Online Family Tree

If you don't already have a genealogical database, you can use the free online version at Ancestry.com. One benefit of filling out an online tree at Ancestry.com is that the site can offer research hints based on the information you enter. Follow these steps to create a family tree:

1. Point your web browser to www.ancestry.com.

2. In the upper-left corner of the home page, click the Family Trees button to open the Family Trees page.

3. Near the top of the page, enter your first name and last name and select your gender, as shown in Figure 2-1.

4. Click the Start Your Tree button. The page that opens displays a three-generation pedigree chart, as shown in Figure 2-2. The first generation contains your name.

5. Add the name of a family member to the tree by clicking the Add Spouse link, the Add Father link, or the Add Mother link. In the pop-over box that appears, enter the first and middle names, maiden (or last) name, gender, birth date, birthplace, and, if applicable, death date and death place. Click the Save button when you finish.

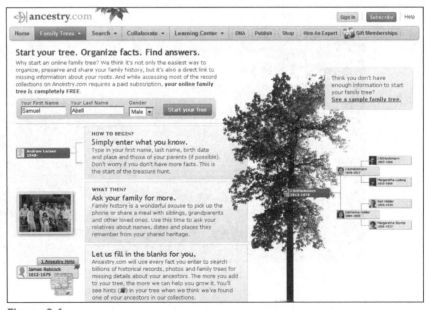

Figure 2-1

Figure 2-2

 When you begin to enter a location in the Birth Place field, a list of potential matching locations appears beneath the field. You can select from the list to enter the information more quickly. You can also use this list to standardize the location that makes searches easier in the Ancestry.com database.

6. In the Save and Build Your Free Family Tree pop-over box that appears, enter a name for your tree and then your e-mail address. If you don't want the tree available to other site users, deselect the Allow Others to View This Tree check box. When you're finished, click the Save My Tree button. The First Name and Last Name fields are then populated with your name.

 Before you save your family tree, be sure to read the Ancestry.com privacy policy that's available on the page.

7. If your e-mail address matches as a registered user of Ancestry.com, the Provide a Password page appears. Type your existing password to continue. If your e-mail address is new to the site, you're automatically registered with Ancestry.com and a default username and password are created.

 To change the default username and password (which you aren't likely to remember), click the link to change your username and password. The family tree you just created is displayed.

8. Add information about other family members by clicking the Add Father, Add Mother, or Add Relative links. Clicking any of these links opens a pop-over box. Enter the individual's first name, middle name, last name, gender, birth date, birthplace, death date, and death place. Click the Save button when you're finished.

9. The pedigree page is shown again, with the names of the new family members on it. If you see the green shaky leaf symbol, as shown in Figure 2-3, Ancestry.com has found a hint. (The symbol might also be accompanied by a

pop-up box explaining the purpose of the leaf symbol. A *pop-up box* is a little message that appears whenever you hover the cursor over a screen element, such as the leaf symbol. If you see a pop-up box, click the See Hint button.) Click the leaf symbol to see the hint. When you finish reading the hint, click the gray box labeled Return to Tree.

Click to view the hint.

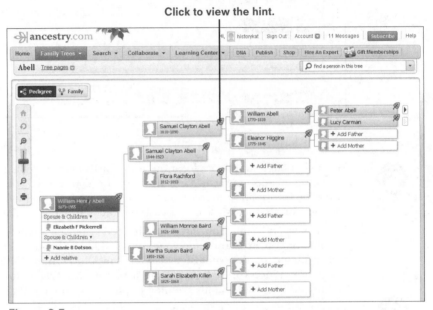

Figure 2-3

Not every individual triggers a hint, so don't be concerned if you don't see one. If you follow a hint that leads to a database that's part of the paid subscription database, the site prompts you to subscribe to the Ancestry.com site. We show you how to receive a free, two-week subscription to the site in Chapter 5.

10. As time allows, add more generations to your family tree.

Adding Facts to a Profile

Your ancestors' life stories consist of more than simply their names, birth information, and death information. You can add details such as *events* that occurred during their lives (marriages, property owned, and medical issues, for example) to make your family history more interesting. Follow these steps to add a fact or an event to a profile on your family tree:

1. If your family tree isn't onscreen, place the cursor over the Family Trees button at the top of the Ancestry.com home page. A secondary menu drops down, showing the family tree you created. Click the family tree name to display your family tree in Pedigree view.

2. Place the cursor over the name of a person on your family tree.

3. In the pop-up box that appears, click View Profile. Several tabs are available on the Profile screen: Overview, Facts and Sources, Media Gallery, Comments, Hints, and Member Connect. As you might expect, the Overview tab, shown in Figure 2-4, shows a summary of the information contained within the other sections.

Click these tabs to navigate the profile.

Figure 2-4

4. To add information about a fact or an event, select the Facts and Sources tab.

5. Click the Add a Fact button on the right side of the pane. The Add a New Fact or Event page appears.

6. Click the Add a New Fact or Event drop-down box and select an event, as shown in Figure 2-5. The information under the drop-down box changes, depending on the event that you selected.

Figure 2-5

7. Fill out the supplemental information under the drop-down box. Click Submit when you're finished. The fact you've entered appears on the Facts and Sources tab.

Citing Sources

A *source* is any material (book, document, record, or periodical, for example) that provides information for your research. For example, Figure 2-6 shows a source citation that provides evidence for a name and residence. We strongly encourage you to cite the sources of all facts and information that you enter into profiles on your family tree.

Figure 2-6

Keeping track of sources helps you remember where you discovered the information and assists other researchers with retracing your steps. If you find conflicting information later, returning to the source can help you sort out the reliability of your information.

Follow these steps to cite a source for a fact you've added to your tree:

1. Display the profile page for the person you want to cite a source for. (Follow Steps 1–3 in the earlier section "Adding Facts to a Profile.")

2. Click the Facts and Sources tab.

3. Click the Source Citations button, which is located just under the Facts and Sources tab.

4. Click the Add a Source Citation link on the right. The Create Source Citation Information page appears.

5. Click the Create a New Source link under Step 1 on the screen. The Create a New Source page appears, as shown in Figure 2-7.

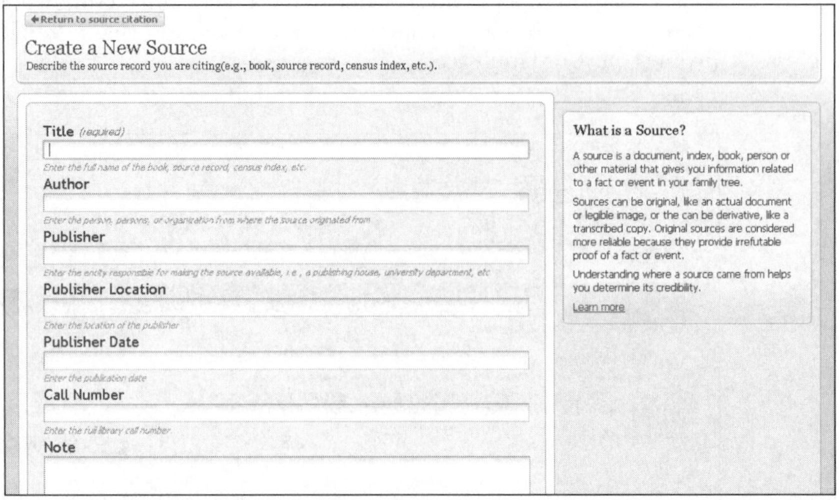

◆ Return to source citation

Create a New Source
Describe the source record you are citing(e.g., book, source record, census index, etc.).

Title (required)

Enter the full name of the book, source record, census index, etc.

Author

Enter the person, persons, or organization from where the source originated from

Publisher

Enter the entity responsible for making the source available, i.e., a publishing house, university department, etc.

Publisher Location

Enter the location of the publisher

Publisher Date

Enter the publication date

Call Number

Enter the full library call number

Note

What is a Source?

A source is a document, index, book, person or other material that gives you information related to a fact or event in your family tree.

Sources can be original, like an actual document or legible image, or the can be derivative, like a transcribed copy. Original sources are considered more reliable because they provide irrefutable proof of a fact or event.

Understanding where a source came from helps you determine its credibility.

Learn more

Figure 2-7

6. Fill out fields for the source of the information. You don't have to fill out all fields — the only required field is Title.

7. Near the bottom of the page, click the Create a New Repository link. A *repository* is a place that holds the source that you're citing, such as a library or a person's house, in the case of the location of family photos.

8. On the Create a New Repository page, fill out the fields to describe the repository. When you're finished, click the Save Repository button to save the repository and return to the Create a New Source page. (Refer to Figure 2-7.) Note that after you've created a repository once, it's then available for you to use in future citations.

9. Click the Save Source button to finish citing the source. The source title is now reflected in the drop-down box under Step 1 on the Create Source Citation Information page.

10. Complete the fields under the Citation portion of the source (Step 2 on the screen). The Detail field is the only required field in this section.

11. If you have a scanned document or an audio recording or a video recording that you want to include as part of the source, click the Yes radio button under Step 3.

12. Under Step 4, select the box next to the fact or event that you want the source to document.

13. When you're finished, click the Save Source Citation button.

Adding Media

To provide more substance to your sources, consider adding media. You can add four types of media: photos, stories, audio recordings, and video recordings. For example, you can scan a birth record of an ancestor and add the record as part of your source citation. Follow these requirements to upload media to Ancestry.com:

- **Photo:** A photo must be in one of these formats: .bmp, .gif, .jpeg, .jpg, .png, or .tiff. No individual photo can be larger than 15 megabytes (MB).
- **Story:** Type the story at the site, or upload it in one of these formats: .doc, .docx, .pdf, .rtf, or .txt. No individual story can exceed 15 megabytes (MB).
- **Audio:** Add audio recordings directly via the Ancestry.com site.
- **Video:** A video recording must be shot using a webcam and recorded using the Ancestry.com site. Videos must be less than 12 minutes long.

Follow these steps to add media to your Ancestry.com family tree:

1. Display your family tree, and then open the personal profile to which you want to add media.
2. Click the Media Gallery tab.
3. Click the Add Media button on the right side of the screen. On the drop-down menu shown in Figure 2-8, you can choose to upload media from your computer (either a photo or a text file or a word processing file), type a story, record audio, or record video.

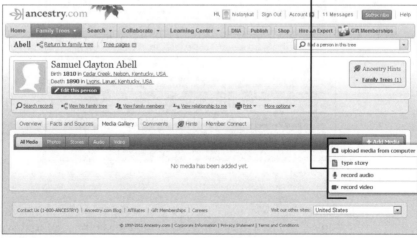

Figure 2-8

4. Select Upload Media from Computer. The Upload Media page appears, as shown in Figure 2-9.

Figure 2-9

5. Click the Content Submission Agreement link. Read the submission agreement, shown in Figure 2-10, so that you know the terms and limitations of posting content to the Ancestry.com site. Click the Close box (the X in the upper-right corner of the pop-up screen) to close the content submission agreement.

Figure 2-10

6. Select the check box labeled I Accept the Content Submission Agreement only if you have read the agreement and you're comfortable with its terms

and conditions. If you choose not to accept it, you cannot submit media to Ancestry.com.

7. Click the Select Files button. The Open dialog box appears.

8. Select the files you want to upload, and then click the Open button. While the files are being uploaded, you should see the progress bar on your screen. After the upload is complete, the Add Details to Your Media page opens, as shown in Figure 2-11.

Figure 2-11

 To select multiple files to upload at the same time, hold down the Ctrl key in Windows or the Command key on the Mac.

9. Replace the title of the image in the Title field. (The Title field must be filled in.) The default title is the filename of the imported image. The filename isn't always a descriptive title, so feel free to make the name more meaningful.

10. Change the category type in the drop-down box, if necessary.

11. Fill in the Date, Location, and Description fields, if you have this information.

12. If you want to attach the media to send to additional people, click the Attach to Another Person link and enter the person's name in the box that appears. For example, if you want to attach a family photograph with a number of people in it who are in your family tree, attach the photo to the names of the appropriate individuals.

 When you begin typing, the name begins to fill in, based on the people in your family tree. You can also click the Browse List link and then select the individual from the list of individuals in the family tree.

13. Click the Save Added Information button. The photo should show up as a thumbnail image in the Media Gallery. Of course, if the media isn't a photo, you see a different icon in the Media Gallery, such as a microphone labeled *Audio* for an audio file.

You can also add the new media to a Fact and Event entry by clicking the Fact & Events button and then the Add Media link on the right side of the event, as shown in Figure 2-12.

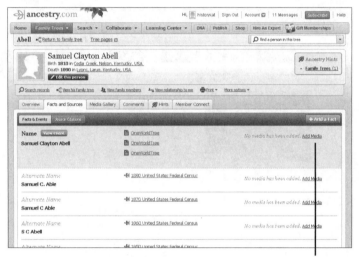

Click to add media.

Figure 2-12

Leaving Comments for Visitors

If you decide to make your family tree available to your family or to other researchers, you might want to leave a comment about a particular ancestor, especially if you want to clarify information about that person. For example, you can explain that the individual whose real name is George was known as Shorty. You can also explain any discrepancy in sources — for example, how an individual's name may have been misspelled on a census record.

Note that comments placed on the records of living people aren't viewable unless you give permission for others to see living individuals in your tree.

Follow these steps to leave a comment on your tree:

1. Display your family tree in Pedigree view, and then open the personal profile to which you want to add a comment.
2. Select the Comments tab, as shown in Figure 2-13.
3. Fill in the Subject and Comment fields.
4. When you're finished, click the Add Comment button.

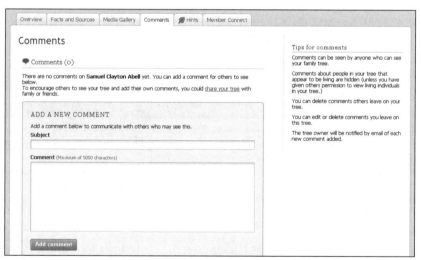

Figure 2-13

Reviewing Hints

One benefit of placing information in an online family tree at Ancestry.com is that you can use *ancestry hints*, which are designed to point you to records contained within the Ancestry.com site that might provide further evidence or documentation about your ancestor. The hints are maximized when you have a subscription to Ancestry.com, but they also can be used to point you in the direction of record sets, even when you have no subscription.

You can review hints by following these steps:

1. Display your family tree, and then open the personal profile for which you want to review hints.

2. Select the Hints tab. The hints page, shown in Figure 2-14, appears, listing record sources that contain a potential match with your ancestor:

- The first column is the name of the record source.

- The second column contains information about the particular record containing your ancestor's name. Note that this column doesn't provide all the information that might be contained within the record; however, it gives you an idea of the *type* of information that matched the record with your ancestor.

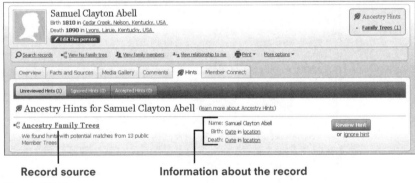

Record source   **Information about the record**

Figure 2-14

3. Click the Review Hint button to take a closer look at the record. If you have a subscription to Ancestry.com, you see more information about the record. If you don't have a subscription, you see a splash page that advertises membership and explains how to start a free, two-week trial. (See Chapter 5 for details on starting your trial subscription.)

4. If the hint isn't valid for your ancestor, click the Ignore Hint link.

Ignoring the hint doesn't delete it from the profile. The hint is moved to the Ignored Hints page, where you can review it again by clicking the Ignored Hints button.

Connecting with Other Members

To make the most of your Ancestry.com membership, initiate contact and share information with other members who are researching your ancestors. From the profile page, you can do this on the Member Connect tab. The Member Connect feature actively looks for other people who are posting information about your ancestor on their online family trees. After finding a potential match, Member Connect lists the member's name on the tab.

To find members who are researching one of your ancestors, follow these steps:

1. Display your family tree, and then open the profile for which you want to search for member activity.

2. Select the Member Connect tab to see possible connections for this ancestor, as shown in Figure 2-15.

Figure 2-15

3. To contact another Ancestry.com member, click the username next to the Added By title. Then click the Contact button, and type the subject and message. Clicking the Send button sends the message directly to the user. You must be a subscribing member at Ancestry.com to be able to contact another member.

Ancestry.com subscribers see links to the family trees containing the related information about the ancestor. Nonsubscribers see only the number of records, sources, and photos that are available on that family tree.

Chapter 3

Building Your Family Tree with RootsMagic

Several varieties of software can help you organize your genealogical records and research and help you create attractive charts, trees, and reports. In one variety of software, the *genealogical database,* you can store specific facts about people and associate those people into relationships. A few genealogy databases companies offer a free, limited version of their software. These include Legacy Standard Version (www.legacyfamilytree.com), Gramps (gramps-project.org), Family Tree Legends (www.familytreelegends.com), and Personal Ancestral File (www.familysearch.org/eng/paf/). In this chapter, we chose to cover another popular package, RootsMagic Essentials, which contains a good selection of tools to give you a flavor of the capabilities of genealogical software.

Of course, you may already own or prefer a different genealogical database, such as Family Tree Maker or Master Genealogist for Windows or Reunion by Leisterpro for the Mac. You can still follow these steps to try RootsMagic Essentials for free, or you can follow similar steps to perform the same actions in your preferred database.

tech 2 to connect

activities

- Installing RootsMagic Essentials
- Entering family data
- Citing all your sources
- Generating a family tree chart
- Creating a GEDCOM to export your data

Installing RootsMagic Essentials

Download and install the free trial version of RootsMagic Essentials software by following these steps:

1. Open your web browser, and go to the RootsMagic site at `http://roots magic.com/Products`.

2. Scroll down to the second section, labeled RootsMagic Essentials, and click the Free Download button, as shown in Figure 3-1.

Figure 3-1

3. Complete the information fields, if you want: First Name, Last Name, and E-Mail. Enter your e-mail address again in the Verify E-Mail field.

4. Select the check box if you want to receive news and updates from RootsMagic via e-mail.

5. Click the Download button. The instructions for downloading the product appear.

6. Click the RootsMagic Essentials Installer link. The File Download dialog box appears and asks, "Do you want to run or save this file?"

7. Click the Run button. The progress bar shows the status of the download as it progresses. The software downloads to your computer. When the download is complete, the Welcome to RootsMagic Setup Wizard opens.

Depending on your computer's operating system, a security warning may appear and ask whether you truly want to continue installing or running the program. Click Run or Continue to continue. If you click the Don't Run button, the software isn't installed, and you must use another genealogical database to complete the remaining steps and activities in this chapter.

8. In the Welcome to RootsMagic Setup Wizard dialog box, click Next. The license agreement appears.

9. Scroll down to read the entire licensing agreement. If you agree to its terms, select the I Accept the Agreement option and click Next. In the window that appears, you can choose whether to have the program create an icon for launching it.

10. Click Install. The installation progress bar appears, and the software installs on your computer. When the installation is complete, the Completing the RootsMagic Setup Wizard box appears.

11. To open RootsMagic now, select the Launch RootsMagic check box and click the Finish button. A window opens, welcoming you to the software and asking you to identify which version of the product you're opening.

12. Click the RootsMagic Essentials Free Version link. The RootsMagic News and Updates dialog box opens, with links to more information about the software. If you don't want to see similar items when using RootsMagic Essentials, select the Do Not Show Me This Again check box. Otherwise, simply click the Close button.

Entering Family Data

The easiest way to use your genealogical database (RootsMagic Essentials or another program) is to start entering information that you know about yourself, your spouse, and your children and then work backward through generations of your ancestors, including your parents, grandparents, and great-grandparents.

After you complete your direct lines as far back as you can, enter information about each of your siblings, nieces, nephews, cousins, and other relatives. Always enter as much information as you can in the fields in the Add Person dialog boxes.

When you finish installing the RootsMagic Essentials software, you see the Welcome to RootsMagic dialog box, shown in Figure 3-2, with four options listed.

Figure 3-2

Use the options in the Welcome dialog box to enter data about your family in Steps 1–3 (if you're returning to RootsMagic Essentials after a break from the preceding activity, continue at Step 4):

1. Click the Create link. The New File dialog box appears, as shown in Figure 3-3.

2. Enter the new filename in the New File Name field, and set the optional formatting items that you want, including the date format of the file and whether to display a number after a name, display surnames in all capital letters, and set up and support certain additional fields for the Latter-day Saints. Then specify whether you're starting a new file or importing an existing one.

    To name the file, consider using the surname of the ancestor who is the primary focus of the file. For example, when you're starting with yourself, you can use your surname as the filename.

3. Click OK. The database is created, and Pedigree view opens, as shown in Figure 3-4.

Figure 3-3

Click here to start entering info.

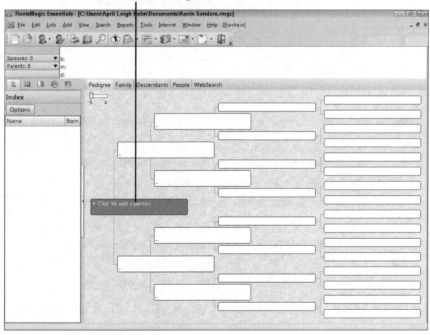

Figure 3-4

4. In Pedigree view, select the Click to Add a Person box. The Add Person dialog box appears, as shown in Figure 3-5, where you can fill in details about yourself or an ancestor.

Figure 3-5

5. Type your first and middle names in the Given Name(s) field, and type your last name in the Surname field. Then complete the remaining fields to the extent that you know the data that belongs in them. When you're finished, click OK.

Enter your maiden name if you're female, regardless of your marital status, and enter the four-digit year for dates in RootsMagic. If you inadvertently use only two numerals for the year, the software accepts the year as is, leaving it ambiguous for anyone who references your database.

6. In the Edit Person dialog box, shown in Figure 3-6, add more facts about yourself or an ancestor by clicking one of these five buttons in the edit window: Note or Sources in the lower-right corner or Address, Media, or To Do along the top of the dialog box. After you finish adding details, click Save.

Add or delete facts by clicking the Add a Fact button (the green plus sign) or the Delete Fact button (the red X), respectively, to open the Fact Types dialog box, shown in Figure 3-7.

7. Click Close to return to Pedigree view.

8. After you enter the name of the first person, click the name of the next person whose information you want to complete, or click the Add People to the Database icon on the toolbar. Enter information for people related to the individual, such as a spouse, children, or parents.

Click to add or delete facts.

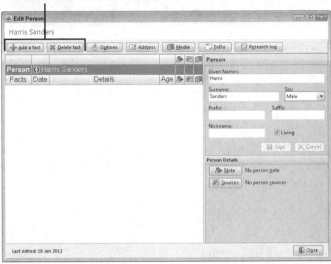

Figure 3-6

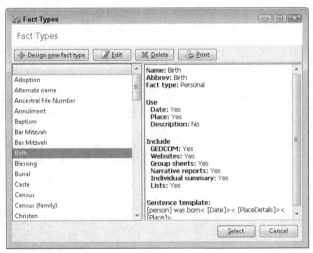

Figure 3-7

Citing All Your Sources

When you're researching your family history, it's important to *source* your data (record the origins of all data you're collecting) so that you know where to return for clarification or additional information if questions arise. Sourcing also validates your research if you intend to use it for scholarly purposes or to apply for certain society memberships.

Citing data sources as you enter information about people is the easiest method. Most genealogical software programs, including RootsMagic Essentials, let you enter source information. To cite a source in RootsMagic Essentials, follow these steps:

1. From Pedigree view, double-click the person that the source references. For example, if you're citing the source of information about your marriage and you have a copy of your marriage certificate, you would double-click your name in the Pedigree view.

2. Highlight the fact or event that you want to source. For example, highlight the marriage fact in the left side of the box.

3. Click the Sources button near the bottom of the right pane. The Citation Manager opens for the fact you chose in Step 2.

4. Click the Add New Source button. The Select Source Type dialog box appears.

5. Select a source type from the Source Type list. For example, in Figure 3-8, we selected Marriage Record (Civil).

6. Click OK. The Edit Source dialog box appears, as shown in Figure 3-9. You can enter detailed information about the record and its repository (where the source is stored).

7. Complete as many fields as you want for the source, and then click OK. You should see a check mark under the Source icon in the Edit Person box.

As an alternative way to open the Citation Manager box, choose Lists⇨Source List from the menu bar. Using this method, you can enter data for general sources that apply to more than one type of information or event. This method is also helpful for recording a memoir, diary, or letter from an ancestor.

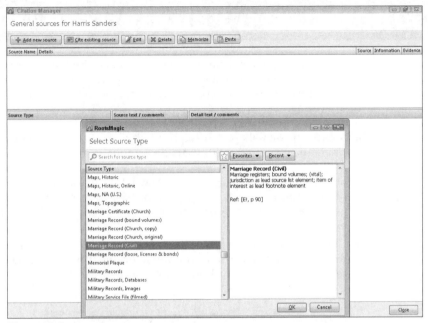

Figure 3-8

Figure 3-9

Generating a Family Tree Chart

At some point, you may want to produce an attractive family tree to share with others, perhaps for a family reunion or to send to another relative who is researching the same family or simply to include in a paper-based book that you're writing.

In this activity, we walk you through the steps to generate a family tree by using the data you've entered in RootsMagic Essentials:

1. Start from Pedigree view in RootsMagic Essentials, and highlight the name of the person who will serve as the focus of your report. For example, if your great-grandfather is the central point of the report, highlight the box with his name in it.

2. Choose Reports⇨Pedigree Chart from the menu bar. The Report Settings dialog box appears, where you can determine which information to include in the chart and how it should look (see Figure 3-10).

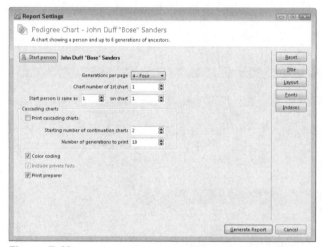

Figure 3-10

Some report types aren't available in the RootsMagic Essentials version. You have to purchase the full product to generate them.

3. Verify the name to the right of the Start Person button. To change the name, click the Start Person button and then select the correct person.

4. Select the number of generations to include, and determine the remaining chart settings, such as chart number, placement of focal person on the chart, whether the chart should cascade, and how many generations to include.

5. Using the buttons on the right side, you can also specify the settings for other features of the chart, including the title, print layout, and font and whether to generate an index.

6. After you complete all settings, click the Generate Report button. RootsMagic Essentials generates the report and displays it on your screen, as shown in Figure 3-11. You can then print it or adjust the settings to change how it looks.

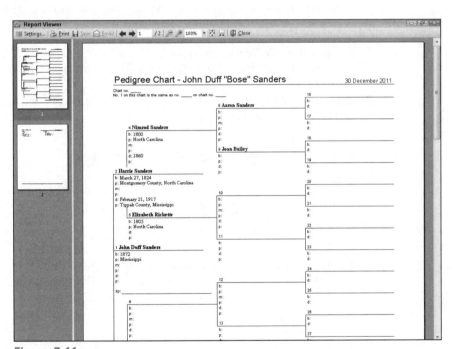

Figure 3-11

Creating a GEDCOM File to Export Your Data

To help genealogists more easily share data between different types of genea-logical databases (because *no one* wants to retype the same data in multiple soft-ware programs), the Church of Jesus Christ of Latter-day Saints (LDS) released *GEDCOM* in 1984. This *ge*nealogical *d*ata *com*munication specification is simply a uniform file format that individuals and software manufacturers use to export and import data among various genealogical databases.

If you want to share information with other researchers you know, you should know how to create your own GEDCOM file, using RootsMagic Essentials. Follow these steps:

1. Starting from Pedigree view in RootsMagic Essentials, click the name of the ancestor who is furthest back in the family tree that you want to export in a GEDCOM file.

2. Choose File⇨Export from the menu bar. The GEDCOM Export dialog box opens, as shown in Figure 3-12.

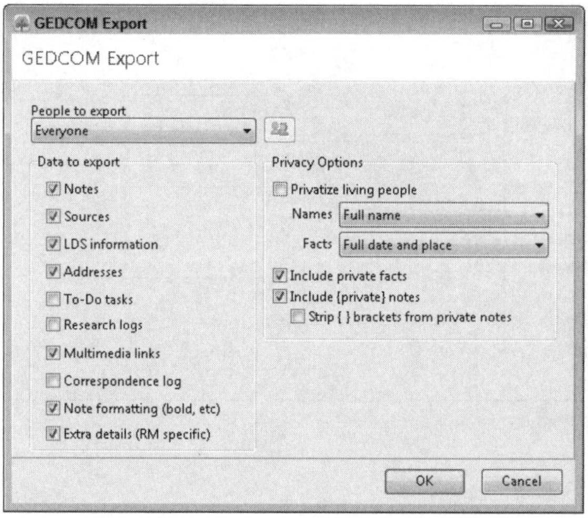

Figure 3-12

3. From the People to Export drop-down list, choose the Everyone option to include everyone in the database or choose the Select from List option to specify which people to include.

4. Pick items to include from the Data to Export section, including notes, sources, and addresses.

5. Select settings in the Privacy Options section, where you can specify whether to privatize the information and to what extent (excluding living people or facts).

6. Click OK. The Save As dialog box opens.

7. Enter the name of the GEDCOM file in the File Name field, navigate to the location on your computer where you want to store the file, and then click Save.

After you create the GEDCOM file, you can attach it via e-mail or open it in a word processor, as shown in Figure 3-13, to print a copy of it.

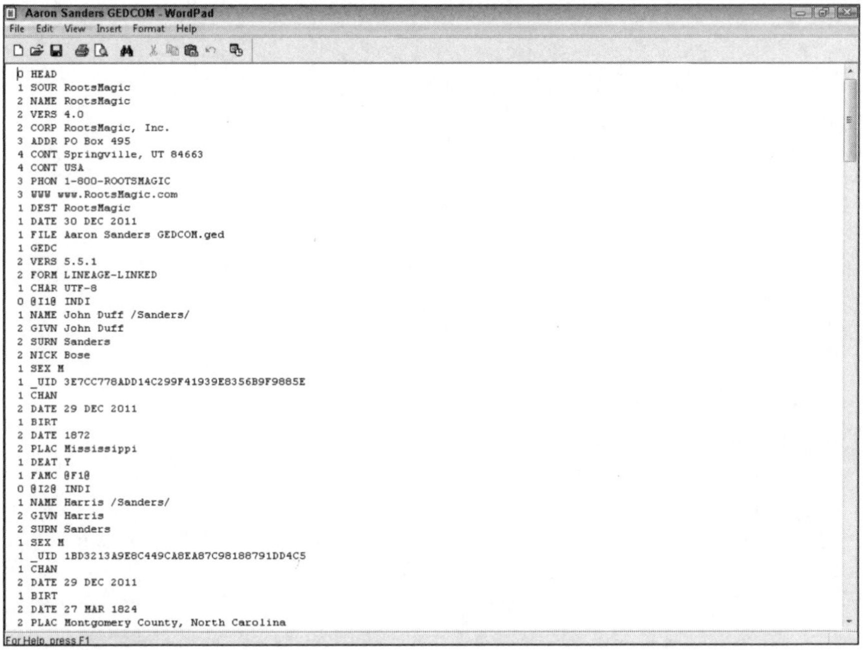

Figure 3-13

Chapter 4

Using Web Search Engines

It doesn't take long to realize that a seemingly endless amount of information is available at your fingertips on the Internet. As with almost any subject, an overabundance of sites claim content that's of interest — and of use — to family history research. To sort through all these sites and weed out the ones that are irrelevant to your genealogy research, you typically turn to a search engine, such as Google, Bing, Yahoo!, Dogpile, or Ask.com.

Using a search engine is definitely more of an art than a science. You may find that a search term you use to locate records about one ancestor may not work exactly the same way when you're looking for another ancestor, because the data differs among the millions of websites that are indexed by search engines. Likewise, because every search engine works differently, the way you use one to search may not work at another search engine site.

activities

tech to connect

- Searching for phrases at Google
- Targeting your search using Google
- Learning additional search tricks
- Comparing results at Bing
- Using metasearch engines
- Performing genealogically focused searches

Searching for Phrases at Google

The most straightforward strategy in picking a phrase to search for is to use your ancestor's name. Depending on the name, you may see a few matches — or millions of matches — in the search engine. We show you how this process works at the extremely popular Google search site, and then we show you how to modify the search phrase *slightly* to see the search results change.

Follow these steps to search for a phrase at Google:

1. Open your web browser and go to Google at `www.google.com`.

2. Click the Search field directly below the Google logo, and type an ancestor's name. To help illustrate the changes you'll cause by modifying the search phrase, start by using a name that isn't unique so that you're likely to see at least a hundred matches. We entered the name *John Sanders* — the name of April's grandfather and great-grandfather, as shown in Figure 4-1.

Search button

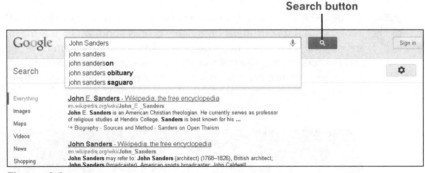

Figure 4-1

As you type, Google makes suggestions regarding your search phrase and tries to finish the phrase for you. If you want, you can select a suggested phrase by clicking it.

3. Click the Google Search button. Google quickly skims its database and returns a list of potential matches to your search phrase. More than 5 million hits were returned on the name John Sanders. Five million hits are too many to browse, so restrict the search to reduce the number of results.

4. Click in the Search field (now at the top of the page), and add another word or two related to your ancestor, such as a middle or maiden name, a location, or a birth year or death year. In our example, we added the middle name *Duff* and the location *Texas*.

5. Click the Search button. In a matter of seconds, Google compiles a new list of results that is more restricted than the first. As you can see in Figure 4-2, our results for the phrase *John Duff Sanders Texas* cut the number of results for *John Sanders* by half. And the first few results in the list look quite promising. However, more than 3.2 million potential matches are still too many to browse; the list should be reduced even further.

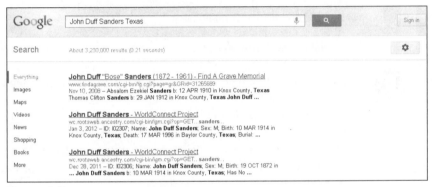

Figure 4-2

6. Click in the Search field again, and enclose the name of your ancestor in quotation marks. For example, we entered *"John Duff Sanders" Texas*.

Enclosing a phrase in quotation marks tells Google to look for an exact match to your search term. They weed out any results where all names appear on a site but not necessarily next to or in relation to each other.

7. Click Search. Google searches again and creates a new list of results. This time, the search example drops from more than 3 million hits to 352 potential matches. This number of sites is much more manageable to review, especially considering that we're likely to rule out visits to sites based on abstracts provided by Google. (An *abstract* is a snippet of an indexed website that provides context where search terms are found.)

8. Scroll the list and click any link that looks promising to visit its website.

Targeting Your Search Using Google

The search in the preceding activity helps you get your feet wet using a search engine. You can form a reasonable estimate of the number and types of websites that are available for your family history research. But making a simple search may still yield too many results to handle realistically or efficiently or may yield results that aren't helpful to your pursuits because they don't contain the types of information you need or data for the appropriate people, locations, or events. You should restrict the results even further based on additional information. To use the advanced search features of Google, follow these steps:

1. Point your web browser to www.google.com/advanced_search. The Advanced Search page opens.

   Alternatively, first type your search term in the box, and then click the Advanced Search link at the bottom of the page.

2. In the first section, Find Pages With, enter the words you're looking for. This list describes when to use the available fields:

   - *All These Words:* When the words can appear in any order or context.

   - *This Exact Word or Phrase:* When you're typing a name or location that needs to match the exact order.

   - *Any of These Words:* When you want Google to look for any site that might have one of many words (such as location names within a state or county). You can see an example of our advanced search for April's ancestors in Figure 4-3. We're looking for sites that have death-related information in three locations in Texas for an ancestor named John Duff Sanders.

   - *None of These Words:* When you don't want to see certain words in your search results. For example, you can exclude commonplace names that appear often in search results but don't relate to your search. If a website contains these words, Google omits them from the results.

3. Enter any additional parameters for your search in the Then Narrow Your Results By section:

   - *Language:* Choose the language for your results. (Any Language is the default, so if a website uses a language other than English, you see it in its native language.)

   - *Region:* Restrict by region.

   - *Last Update:* Indicate how recently the website was created or updated.

- *Site or Domain:* Restrict the search to a particular domain or website.
- *Terms Appearing:* Specify where on the website your search terms appear (such as whether the name appears in the title, text, or links).
- *Safe Search:* Turn off or on Safe Search (a filter to omit possibly objectionable content).
- *File Type:* Indicate whether you want to see results in only a particular type of file.
- *Usage Rights:* Specify whether a license is required to use the site (for example, whether you have to pay to view or update the site).

4. When you finish entering search criteria, click the Advanced Search button. Google uses the Advanced Search terms to generate a list of results.

5. Scroll the list of results, and if a site looks like it might have information pertaining to your ancestor, click the link to go see it.

Figure 4-3

Learning Additional Search Tricks

The Advanced Search functions at most major search engine sites usually restrict or expand searches enough to generate a decent list of results. However, you might find a few more tricks useful. Like quote marks (which we cover in the first activity in this chapter), the punctuation marks described in the following list can be used in the simple Search fields — they don't require you to use the more complicated Advanced Search forms:

- **Asterisk:** Serves as a wildcard term
- **Parentheses:** Distinguishes conditions for searching
- **Minus sign:** Excludes certain words or terms
- **Two periods:** Indicate a range of numbers, such as years

Follow these steps to see how to use these four tricks to expand or reduce search results:

1. Go to Google at www.google.com.

2. Click in the Search field, and type the first and last names of an ancestor between quotation marks so that Google looks for the names as one phrase. (We use *John Sanders* again.)

3. Click the Search button. Google generates a list of results. In our example, Google found more than 5 million potential matches.

4. If you need to expand your list of results, try adding the wildcard term in the form of an asterisk (*). If you place a wildcard between the first and last names, Google looks for anyone who has those first and last names but any or no middle name. For example, if our list isn't expansive enough, we can insert an asterisk (like this — *"John * Sanders"*) so that Google looks for any John Sanders, including those who have another name between their first and last names.

5. Click Search and watch the list of results grow. In the example, our search results increased to more than 350 million. This number is obviously too many for us to look at, so we omitted the asterisk and reinserted the known middle name for the next part of the activity. Adding the middle name reduces the number of John Sanders results that are returned.

6. If your ancestor's name could have had different spellings, you can use parentheses to set apart a condition to consider multiple spellings and use the word *OR* in the condition. In the example, we know that April's great-grandfather's last name was sometimes spelled with a *u,* so we set up this condition: *"John Duff (Sanders OR Saunders)".*

7. Click Search when you finish updating your search term. Our sample term in Step 6 prompts Google to look for any John Sanders or John Saunders who has the middle name Duff. See Figure 4-4 to see the search term at the top of the screen and the results underneath it.

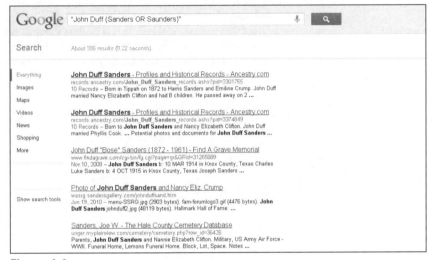

Figure 4-4

8. If Step 7 in this activity results in an unmanageable list of results, you can restrict your search by adding the minus sign (–) and words that you want Google to ignore. For example, in the search results for the name John Sanders (removing the middle name Duff and the condition to consider two spellings for the last name), you can use the minus sign to restrict the search term to exclude any site that contains both *John Sanders* and certain words. Because several of the initial results were for a theologian, a sculptor, and a model and we know that April's ancestor John Sanders was none of these, we added the exclusion so that our search term looks like this: *"John Sanders" – theologian –sculptor –model.*

9. Click Search. Google searches for sites with the name of your ancestor and excludes any site that has the words with the minus sign in front of them.

10. If your ancestor's name was common and the number of your search results is insurmountable, you can use dates and date ranges to restrict the list that Google generates. If you know the precise dates, you can provide a specific year for an event or two years with a hyphen for a lifespan (such as 1872–1961), and Google then uses the dates to limit the results.

If you're unsure of a precise date but you know the general timeframe, you can use two periods (side by side) between two years to prompt Google to look for sites with information about your ancestor between that timeframe. Include a word for the event if you aren't searching using lifespan dates. In keeping with our ongoing John Sanders example, suppose that April doesn't know the year that this ancestor married but believes that it was between 1875 and 1880. She can include these two dates with the two periods between them in her search term so that it looks like this: *"John Sanders" marriage 1875..1880.*

11. Click Search. Figure 4-5 shows you what this search and its results look like.

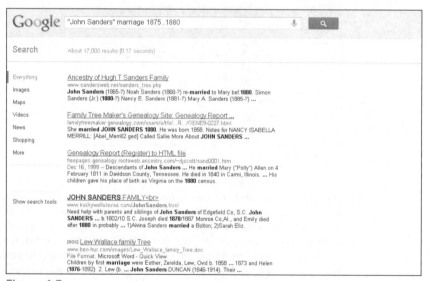

Figure 4-5

Comparing Results at Bing

All previous activities in this chapter use the popular search engine Google. Many other search engines are available, so don't think that you have to use one exclusively. As we mention at the beginning of this chapter, because the search engines are programmed slightly differently, the results from different search engines may vary. To illustrate, follow these steps to repeat a search from the first activity:

1. Direct your web browser to Bing at www.bing.com.

2. Click the Search field next to the Bing logo, and type the name of one of your ancestors (first and last names or first, middle, and last names) and a location associated with this ancestor. We typed the following line in the Search field in our example: *"John Duff Sanders" Texas.*

3. Click the Search icon, which looks like a magnifying glass, to the right of the Search field. Bing searches its database and generates a list of results. Figure 4-6 shows you the results from our example.

Figure 4-6

4. Compare the results at Bing to those from Google in the first activity in this chapter.

Using Metasearch Engines

As you may have already found, multiple search engines are available on the Internet. You can complete individual searches at all of them every time you're looking for information, or you can visit a *metasearch* engine, which compiles the results from multiple search engines. Follow these steps to use a metasearch engine:

1. Point your web browser to Dogpile at www.dogpile.com. Dogpile enables you to search Google, Bing, and Yahoo! at the same time.

2. Click in the Search field in the middle of the page, and type the name of an ancestor (first and last names or first, middle, and last names) and a location associated with this ancestor. (You can use the ancestor from the preceding activity.) As you can see in Figure 4-6, we typed the following line in the Search field in our example: *"John Duff Sanders" Texas*.

3. Click the Go Fetch button. Dogpile fetches matches from the three other search engines and lists the results for you. You might notice that the first few potential matches don't quite match all the terms you entered. Instead, they're sponsored advertisements from the major search engines and, though they don't necessarily contain all your search terms, they're matched to at least one term in your search. See Figure 4-7 for the results we received in the search example.

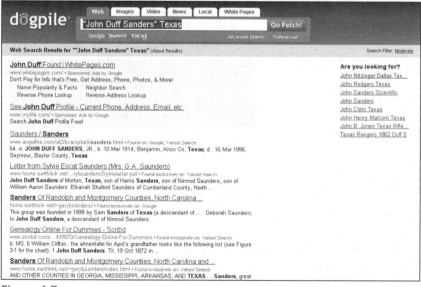

Figure 4-7

4. Scroll the results, and click any links that look promising.

Performing Genealogically Focused Searches

Though you can use general Internet search engines, as described earlier in this chapter, you may find that you prefer genealogically focused searching. Genealogy-focused search engines reduce the amount of browsing and checking you have to do personally by excluding sites that have no information of a family history nature. A couple of examples of genealogically focused search engines are TreEZy (www.treezy.com) and Mocavo (www.mocavo.com).

If your ancestor has a name that has been commonly used by many people over time and it's still rather common, a genealogically focused engine can be extremely helpful. It eliminates your need to sort through articles, advertisements, and postings with information about current people, and it reduces the number of unnecessary sites, such as those that simply link to someone else's website where the name resides.

Using a genealogically focused search engine is similar to using a general search engine. Here's what to do:

1. Point your web browser to Mocavo at www.mocavo.com.

2. Click in the Search field in the middle of the page, and type the name of an ancestor (first and last names or first, middle, and last names) and a location associated with this ancestor. (You can use the same ancestor as you used in the preceding activity.) Sticking with the same name from our earlier examples, we entered the following line in the Search field: *"John Duff Sanders" Texas.*

3. Click the Search button. Mocavo searches its database and generates a list of potential matches. The number of results you see at Mocavo should be substantially less than from using exactly the same search terms at a general search engine, such as Google, because Mocavo restricts the types of sites that it includes when it sends its program out to evaluate websites for indexing. As you can see in Figure 4-8, the number of results in our search term example is greatly reduced from 352 at Google to 4 at Mocavo.

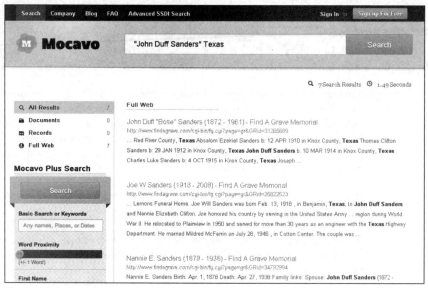

Figure 4-8

4. Scroll the results, and click links that look promising.

Chapter 5

Exploring Ancestry.com

If you want to be successful in tracing your family history online, eventually you'll encounter the resources at Ancestry.com. This for-profit site charges a subscription fee for its most important resources. The company occasionally offers the free use of certain record sets at different times of the year and for special occasions, so check its website frequently — especially around holidays.

A primary benefit of using Ancestry.com is its collection of *digitized* records, which allow you to see representations of original records that you can then interpret as evidence that your ancestor was involved in certain events. Ancestry.com also provides indexes of its original records, to help you find ancestors more quickly than by skimming book indexes or scanning records line-by-line. By using the search engine at the website, also a time-saver, you can search for a single ancestor across multiple record sets. By using this method, you may even encounter your ancestors in record sets where you never expected to find them.

tech 2 to connect

activities

- Initiating the free trial
- Searching all records
- Dealing with search results
- Browsing the card catalog
- Messaging other genealogists
- Learning more about genealogy
- Exploring the wiki

Initiating the Free Trial

If you don't have a subscription to Ancestry.com but you want to find out what kinds of resources it has, try the 14-day free trial before subscribing, to see whether the site is worthwhile. Follow these steps to sign up:

1. Point your web browser to www.ancestry.com.

2. In the upper-right corner of the home page is a green box labeled *14-Day Free Trial*. Click the Give Me Access link in the box. The resulting page contains a table with six subscription options, as shown in Figure 5-1.

Figure 5-1

3. In the Monthly Membership column, click the U.S. Discovery radio button.

Select the monthly membership so if you forget to cancel before the free trial ends, you'll be billed for the least expensive plan. Three-month and 6-month memberships are billed in single payments, so the least amount of risk is in the monthly membership.

Expanding your search beyond the United States

The U.S. version of Ancestry.com offers two types of record sets: U.S. Discovery and World Explorer. As you might expect, the U.S. Discovery version provides access to all U.S. records on the site. The World Explorer version gives you unlimited access to all records on the site — including records from 15 countries outside the United States. If your research interests lie outside the United States, you can use an international flavor of Ancestry.com, such as Ancestry.com.au (Australia), Ancestry.ca (Canada), Jiapu.cn (China), Ancestry.fr (France), Ancestry.de (Germany), Ancestry.it (Italy), Ancestry.se (Sweden), or Ancestry.co.uk (United Kingdom).

4. Click the Start Free Trial button to continue.

5. If you haven't previously registered, enter your first name, last name, and e-mail address, and click the Continue button. If you're already registered, simply click the Log In Here link.

6. Type a password into the Password field, and click the Continue button.

7. Fill in the account information, including your street address, city, state or province, zip or postal code, country, and phone number. Then click the Continue button.

8. Fill in future payment information, including the Card Type, Card Number, Expiration Date, and Card Security Code fields. Then select the check box next to the terms and conditions. Click the Start Free Trial button.

In the rightmost column, note the How Do I Cancel description of the cancellation process so that you can use it at the end of the trial period if you decide that you don't want to continue with a subscription.

9. The resulting page contains information about your free trial. Write down the expiration date, and then click the Continue button. The resulting page is the main Search page for Ancestry.com.

Searching All Records

The easiest way to search Ancestry.com is by submitting your search from the main search form. When you do so, you receive results from *all* collections rather than from only a single record set. Follow these steps to search for an ancestor:

1. Point your web browser to www.ancestry.com, the Ancestry.com home page, and click the Search button in the toolbar at the top of the page. The Search page appears.

2. In the Search section at the top of the page, type a name into the First & Middle Name(s) and Last Name fields.

3. In the Name a Place Your Ancestor Might Have Lived field, type a place where your ancestor lived the majority of his or her life.

   Because the field is a *type-ahead* field, it suggests locations as you type letters into the field.

4. To refine your search, enter a year in the Estimated Birth Year field.

   If you aren't sure of the exact birth date, use the Calculate It link to find it. Clicking this link generates two fields that ask the age of the person in a particular year.

5. If the name you're searching for is common, you may want to add information to distinguish one person from another. You can add *life events* (such as births, marriages, and deaths) by clicking the Add Life Events link. A new row is created when you click the link, as shown in Figure 5-2.

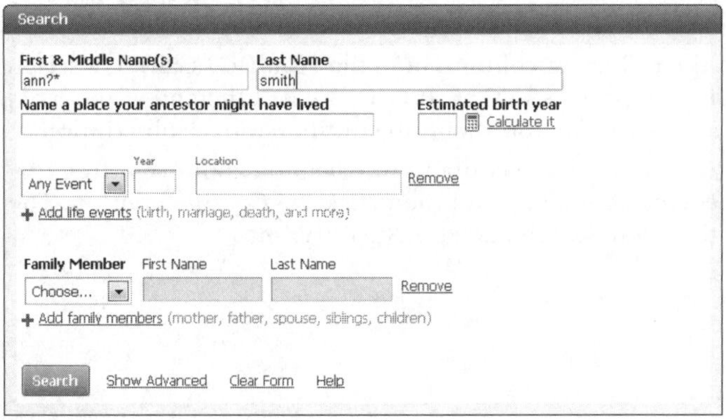

Figure 5-2

Searching for multiple spellings of last names

If you think that your ancestor's name may be misspelled, or spelled multiple ways, use a wildcard in your search — the asterisk (*) or the question mark (?).

The asterisk is used to represent any number of characters. For example, you can type *Will** to search for *Will, Willie,* and *William.* You can also type the asterisk at the beginning of a search. A search for **mogene* might return results such as *Mogene, Emmogene, Emogene, Imogene,* and *Immogene.* The *?* wildcard, on the other hand, represents a single character. For example, you can search for *Dian?* to find both *Diana* and *Diane.* You can also include the asterisk and the question mark in the same search. For example, searching for *Ann?** finds *Anne, Anna,* or *Annabelle* because the question mark signifies at least one more letter after *Ann* and the asterisk indicates that the remaining portion of the name can be any set of letters.

6. Click the down arrow to open the Any Event drop-down menu, and choose the appropriate event type. Enter the year and location of the event. You can add more events by clicking the Add Life Events link again.

7. If you know family members who can be found via your ancestor (such as a parent or spouse), click the Add Family Members link. Then choose the type of family member from the Choose drop-down menu, and complete the individual's First Name and Last Name fields. You can add more people by clicking the Add Family Members link.

8. To add more search criteria, click the Show Advanced link, next to the orange Search button. The expanded search options appear onscreen, as shown in Figure 5-3.

9. You can limit search results to the exact spelling of the name by selecting the Match All Terms Exactly check box at the top of the screen.

10. Click the Use Default Settings link under the First & Middle Name(s) and Last Name fields to configure more search options. The three options described in this list restrict the search on the name:

   - *Phonetic Matches:* The Ancestry.com search engine contains algorithms that determine whether a name sounds like the name you entered into the field.

   - *Names with Similar Meanings or Spellings:* This option is helpful when you search for common first names that are often shortened. For example, Richard is often shortened to Rich, Rick, or Dick.

■ *Records Where Only Initials Are Recorded:* Use this handy option when you search for people who are often referred to by their initials in records, such as A.J. rather than the full name. The Last Name field has an additional choice — to restrict the result to *Soundex* matches (a way of coding names according to the way their consonants sound). When we searched for *Helm* with this check box selected, we received matches for names with the soundex code of H450, including Hellam and Holm, for example.

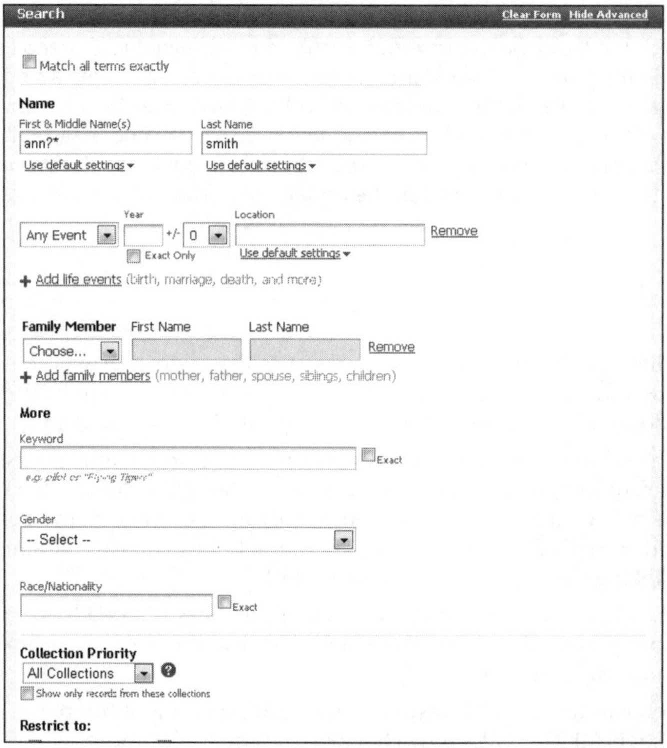

Figure 5-3

11. Click the Use Default Settings link under the Location field to restrict the search to only the location you entered. This option is helpful when you're searching for a common name and you know the location where your ancestor lived. The search then focuses on that person in the context of the location, greatly reducing the number of results.

When you type a place name in the field, additional options appear, including limiting your search to the county/adjacent counties, state, state/adjacent states, or county. Using adjacent counties is particularly helpful when you're searching on counties that were later divided into other counties. The adjacent-counties search picks up the new counties if they're adjacent to the old county.

12. Enter a term into the Keyword field to limit your search to specific criteria. You can use a keyword to search on specific items not covered in the other fields. For example, if you know that your ancestor lived near a specific post office or served in a specific regiment, you can enter that term into the field.

You can further limit the search to the exact term by selecting the Exact check box next to the Keyword field.

13. Click the down arrow in the Gender field, and select the appropriate gender. Choosing the gender is useful when you're searching for an ancestor who has a name that can be either male or female, such as Kelly.

14. Complete the Race/Nationality field. This field is helpful when you search census records in which, depending on the census year, either race or nationality was recorded.

15. Set the collection priority by clicking the arrow on its drop-down menu. The Collection Priority box tells the search engine to give preference in the results to records from a particular country or ethnic group. You can use this option when an ancestor immigrated to a particular country and you want to focus the search on the new country.

By selecting the check box below the Collection Priority drop-down list, you can limit the search to only a particular collection.

16. In the Restrict To section, select one or more check boxes to limit searches to only these elements:

   - Historical records
   - Family trees
   - Stories and publications
   - Photos and maps

We often use the Restrict To functionality to limit searches to only historical records. This way, we restrict the results to records that we can use as evidence — rather than to someone's interpretation of a record in a family tree.

When to use the Match All Terms Exactly option

Use the Match All Terms Exactly option when you know that your ancestor's name is spelled a certain way. For example, the name of Matthew's ancestor Herschel is spelled Heruhel in one record set. To find this record quickly, Matthew would use the Match All Terms Exactly option. Use this functionality also when you're researching a name that's spelled multiple ways and you want to find records with only one spelling. For example, you might want to find only records spelled Smythe and not Smith.

17. After you finish selecting all search options, click the Search button. The search results page appears, as shown in Figure 5-4.

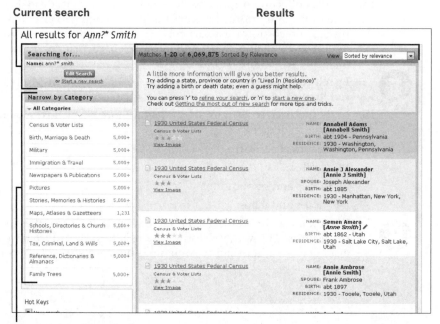

Figure 5-4

Dealing with Search Results

Executing a search is only one step in finding information about an ancestor. The next challenge you face is to manage the hundreds, or perhaps thousands, of results. The search results page is composed of several sections, as described in this list (refer to Figure 5-4):

■ **Searching For:** Located in the upper-left corner and lists the search criteria you used.
■ **Narrow by Category:** Contains categories for displaying results.
■ **Results:** Lists, along the top of the rightmost column, the number of matches and how they're sorted.

Even after adding specific search criteria, you can create a great number of results. For example, a search for *George Helm,* born in 1723 and located in Frederick County, Virginia, yields 84,278 results, if you don't restrict the results in any way. Being able to manage the results is the key to quickly receiving relevant information. To do this, we show you some ways to navigate and view results. Follow these steps:

1. On the search results screen, take a look at the results in the rightmost column. If your search term matches a person in a family tree, that result appears first in the list, as shown in Figure 5-5. The result contains a link to the family tree page and details that are relevant to the individual, such as birth date and birthplace, death date and death place, and parents' names.

MATCHING PERSON (FROM FAMILY TREES)   See more like this

George Helm
Helm Family Tree

BIRTH: 1723 - Frederick, United States
DEATH: 1769 - Winchester, Frederick, Virginia, United States
PARENTS: Leonard Helm, Elizabeth Betty Calmes

Figure 5-5

tech tip

If additional family trees contain information similar to your search, click the See More Like This link on the right side of the Matching Person heading.

2. Along with family tree results, you can see matching records from other sources, including public member photos and scanned documents. Hover the cursor over the link containing the result name. If the result is an Ancestry.com record, the preview box appears, as shown in Figure 5-6. The preview box shows key elements of the record and, possibly, a thumbnail of the record, if it's digitized.

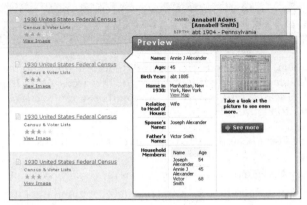

Figure 5-6

3. Sort search results by choosing Summarized by Category from the View drop-down menu in the upper-right corner. This view contains the general record categories followed by the top five sources within these categories, as shown in Figure 5-7.

Click to see all results in the category.

Select an option to sort results.

All results for *Ann?* Smith*

Searching for...		
Name: ann?* smith		
Edit Search		
or Start a new search		

Narrow by Category

⌄ All Categories

Census & Voter Lists	5,000+
Birth, Marriage & Death	5,000+
Military	5,000+
Immigration & Travel	5,000+
Newspapers & Publications	5,000+
Pictures	5,000+
Stories, Memories & Histories	5,000+
Maps, Atlases & Gazetteers	1,231
Schools, Directories & Church Histories	5,000+
Tax, Criminal, Land & Wills	5,000+
Reference, Dictionaries & Almanacs	5,000+
Family Trees	5,000+

Hot Keys

n New search

Matched 6,281,392 from All Categories   View Summarized by category ▾

⌄ **Census & Voter Lists**	380,357
California Voter Registrations, 1900-1968	142,251
1920 United States Federal Census	26,716
1910 United States Federal Census	25,625
1930 United States Federal Census	24,864
1900 United States Federal Census	23,091
See all 380,357 results...	

⌄ **Birth, Marriage & Death**	537,511
Historical Newspapers, Birth, Marriage, & Death Announcements, 1851-2003	79,876
United States Obituary Collection	69,873
England & Wales, FreeBMD Birth Index, 1837-1915	21,676
England & Wales, Death Index: 1916-2005	16,271
The Valley Independent (Monessen, Pennsylvania)	14,420
See all 537,511 results...	

⌄ **Military**	13,208
Stars and Stripes Newspaper, Europe, Mediterranean, and North Africa Editions, 1942-1964	2,671
U.S., Sons of the American Revolution Membership Applications, 1889-1970	1,940
Stars and Stripes Newspaper, Pacific Editions, 1945-1963	1,801
Civil War Pension Index: General Index to Pension Files, 1861-1934	525
List of pensioners on the roll, January 1, 1883, Vols. 1-5	476

Restrict results to a type of record.

Figure 5-7

To see all results in a particular category, click the See All *x* Results link at the bottom of the category.

4. To restrict search results to a particular type of record, select Sorted by Relevance from the View drop-down menu and then click a category in the Narrow by Category section on the left side of the page.

For example, if you select the Census & Voter Lists category, the results screen is filtered to include only the results in that category. Note that the Narrow by Category section changes to a category listing of the census listed by year.

5. If you find a record you're interested in, click the title of the result. The screen turns into the index of the record and lists key details about the individuals in the record, as shown in Figure 5-8.

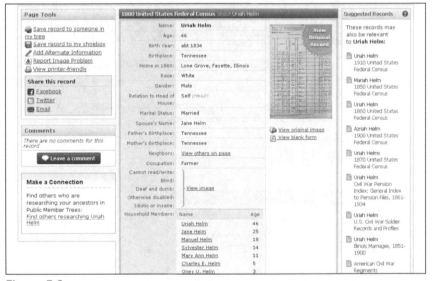

Figure 5-8

6. If the record contains a digitized image, click the thumbnail of the image. (An orange seal labeled *View Original Record* is overlaid on the thumbnail.) The image screen appears, as shown in Figure 5-9.

7. Click the Options button in the green bar above the image. On the pop-up menu that appears, you can switch image viewers, as shown in Figure 5-10. If you have a fast Internet connection, choose the Use the Advanced Viewer option. If you have a slower connection, choose Use Compressed Images.

Expand view
of image.

Print record.

Switch image viewers.

Share record.

Save record to your family tree.

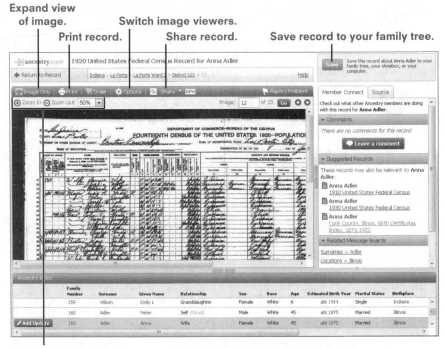

Zoom controls

Figure 5-9

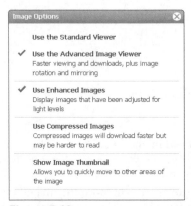

Figure 5-10

If you select a different viewer and the image doesn't appear, click the Options button again and choose Use the Standard Viewer. The Advanced Viewer adds image options, including the Magnify, Rotate, and Mirror functions.

8. You can change the image view onscreen in a couple of ways:

   - *Zoom controls:* Click the Zoom In button (underneath the green bar along the top) to get a closer look at the document. You can also use the percentage zoom drop-down menu to view the image at 50 percent, 100 percent, 150 percent, or 200 percent zoom.

   - *Image Only button:* To see more of the image on the screen, click the Image Only button on the green bar. The screen is resized, and the rightmost column disappears, leaving a wide view of the image. To return to the original image, click the Image Only button on the green bar again to return it to View All status.

9. To print this image, click the Print button. A dialog box appears with print options, as shown in Figure 5-11. Click the button corresponding to your preferred option. A new page is launched with instructions for printing and saving the image. Complete the steps, and close the additional page.

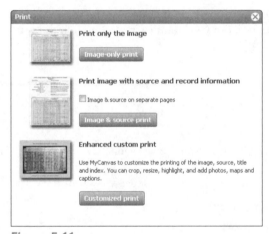

Figure 5-11

10. To share this record with friends or family members, click the Share button on the green bar and then choose the Email option. The Email This to a Friend dialog box opens, as shown in Figure 5-12. Fill in the friend's e-mail address, and add a message, if you prefer. You can also share a link to the image on Facebook or Twitter.

11. If you have an online family tree, click the Save button in the upper-right corner of the screen to add the image to your tree. In the dialog box that opens, select the Attach This Record to Someone In My Tree option and click Continue. (See Chapter 2 for details on creating an online family tree at Ancestry.com.)

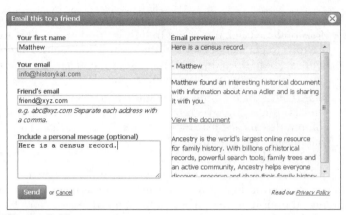

Figure 5-12

12. Click the Attach button next to the name of the person you want to attach the image to. Items from your family tree that match the record appear, as shown in Figure 5-13.

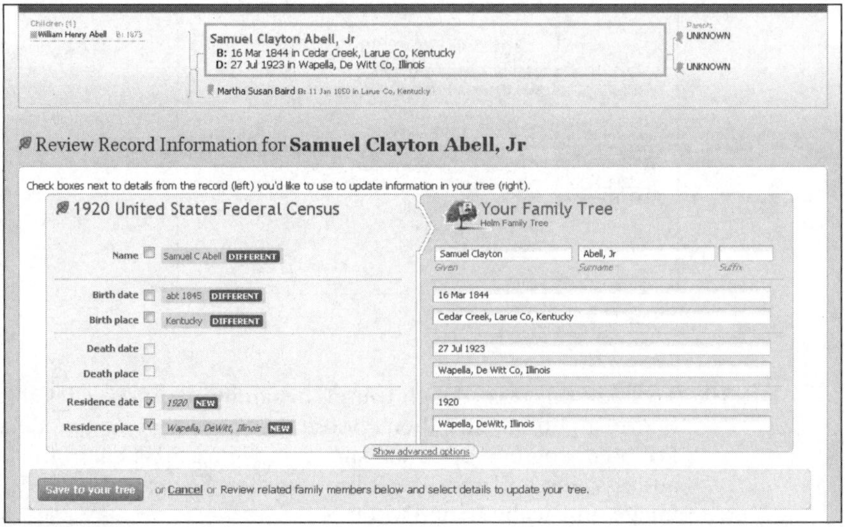

Figure 5-13

13. Pick data elements from the record to add to your family tree by selecting the boxes to the left of the fields.

14. Click the Save to Your Tree button. The screen changes to the main page in your family tree for the person to whom you attached the image. An entry for the record is made in the individual's timeline.

Browsing the Card Catalog

Sometimes you want to research a particular record set rather than search all available records on a particular ancestor. You might also want to see which types of record sets are available for a given period or location. The solution to both research needs is to use the Ancestry Card Catalog. Follow these steps:

1. From the Ancestry.com home page, hover the cursor over the Search button at the top of the page, and select Card Catalog from the drop-down menu. The Ancestry Card Catalog screen appears, showing a list of record sets arranged by popularity.

2. To list titles by date, click the Sort By drop-down list at the top of the results and select Date Updated. This view shows you the most recent databases and those that have new updates, as shown in Figure 5-14.

Figure 5-14

3. To find out more about a record set, place the cursor over the title of the record set. A description of the record pops up on the screen, as shown in Figure 5-15.

Figure 5-15

4. If you want to filter results so that you have fewer to sort, click a link in the left column, in the Filter Titles section. You can filter in one of four ways: by collection, location, date, or language.

5. If you want to search in your results, click the Title field in the Search Titles section (in the upper-left corner), enter a search phrase in the Keyword(s) field, and then click the Search button.

For example, you can type **War of 1812** to see results that contain the phrase *War of 1812* in their titles.

6. Click a title to open the search page for the record set.

Messaging Other Genealogists

At some point in your research, you may need help from other genealogists, perhaps to find information about a particular individual or family or to find out how to research in a particular location. Either way, the message boards at Ancestry.com can help. You can post on them a query that can be read by a number of other researchers, and you can view posts from other researchers who might answer your query. Of course, if you know about a topic on the message board, you can assist other researchers, too.

Follow these steps to collaborate with other members:

1. From the Ancestry.com home page, click the Collaborate button on the toolbar at the top of the page. The Collaborate with Ancestry.com page appears.

2. In the Search the Boards section, in the Names or Keywords field, type a last name, location, or topic and then click the Search button. The resulting page contains posts that other researchers have made that contain your search term, as shown in Figure 5-16.

Figure 5-16

3. Click the title of a post to view its full post contents. The message board page contains the text of the post and, below it, any replies to the post, as shown in Figure 5-17.

Click to start a new thread.   **Click to reply to a post.**

Figure 5-17

4. If you want to reply to a post, click the Reply link at the bottom of the post.

5. To create a new post on a new topic, click the Begin New Thread link. The Post New Thread page appears, as shown in Figure 5-18.

Figure 5-18

6. Enter the appropriate information in the Subject, Message, and Surnames fields, and then click the Post button.

You can also classify your post and upload an attachment that pertains to it.

Learning More about Genealogy

If you're new to family history research or if you want to understand how to better use Ancestry.com resources, the Learning Center may be the place for you — its videos, articles, and tutorials can help speed your research. Follow these steps to explore the Learning Center:

1. From the Ancestry.com home page, click the Learning Center link on the toolbar. The Learning Center page appears, as shown in Figure 5-19.

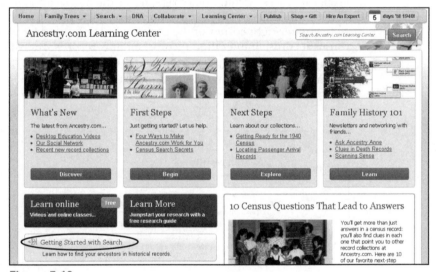

Figure 5-19

2. Near the middle of the page, click the Getting Started with Search link to open the How to Search page. It contains a video and some articles about searching.

3. Click the Play button on the How to Search at Ancestry.com video. The video begins playing. When you have completed the video, you can click the Close (X) box in the upper-right corner of the video screen to close it.

4. Click the Family History 101 tab at the top of the page.

5. Along the left side are how-to articles that can help explain some ways in which genealogical research is conducted. Click on one that looks interesting if you want to learn more about that topic.

Exploring the Wiki

To find more information on research topics, check out the Ancestry.com Family History wiki. A *wiki* is a website where a user can add, modify, and delete content by using a web browser. It's composed of content from two popular books: *The Source: A Guidebook to American Genealogy,* edited by Loretto Dennis Szucs and Sandra Hargreaves Luebking, and *Red Book: American State, County, and Town Sources,* edited by Alice Eichholz. Other relevant content created by Ancestry.com is included in the wiki. Follow these steps to search the wiki:

1. From the Ancestry.com home page, hover the mouse over the Learning Center link, and then choose Family History Wiki from the drop-down menu. In the upper-right corner of the page are links to specific topics such as census records, immigration records, military records, and vital records.

2. In the Search box in the left column, enter your topic and click the Go button. The search results page contains two types of matches — page title and page text, as shown in Figure 5-20.

Figure 5-20

3. Click a topic title to see its full article within the wiki.

Chapter 6

Using FamilySearch

Although *FamilySearch* — the largest free genealogy website — is provided by The Church of Jesus Christ of Latter-day Saints, you don't need to be a member of the church to use the site, and the records extend to those outside the church. The FamilySearch organization has collected, preserved, and shared genealogical records for more than 100 years. Traditionally, these resources were microfilmed and shared by way of the more than 4,500 Family History Centers and the Family History Library in Salt Lake City, Utah. However, this process changed with the introduction of the FamilySearch website on May 24, 1999.

Over the past dozen years, more than 1 billion names have been placed in databases that are available on the website, with more than 1 million registered users and more than 50,000 users per day. Over the past few years, FamilySearch has not only placed its own records online but has also negotiated agreements with commercial genealogy companies to include its content on the site or to link to content on commercial sites.

tech 2 connect

activities

- Creating a FamilySearch account
- Searching historical records
- Browsing by location
- Discovering family trees
- Using the library catalog
- Viewing scanned books
- Volunteering to index

Creating a FamilySearch Account

To be able to benefit from the functionality of the FamilySearch site, you need to create an account. Follow these steps:

1. Set your web browser to www.familysearch.org.

2. In the upper-right corner of the screen, click the Sign In link. The Sign In page appears, as shown in Figure 6-1.

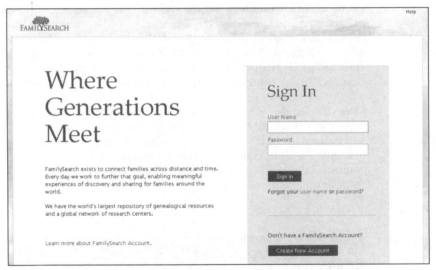

Figure 6-1

3. On the right side of the page, click the Create New Account button. The Registration page opens, as shown in Figure 6-2.

4. Choose the type of account you want to create:

   ▪ *LDS FamilySearch:* Select this option if you're a member of The Church of Jesus Christ of Latter-day Saints. Follow the onscreen prompts to complete your registration.

   ▪ *FamilySearch:* If you aren't a member of the LDS church, select the FamilySearch Account radio button and fill out all fields on the form. When you finish, click the Register button to open a page notifying you that an activation notice was sent to the e-mail address you provided.

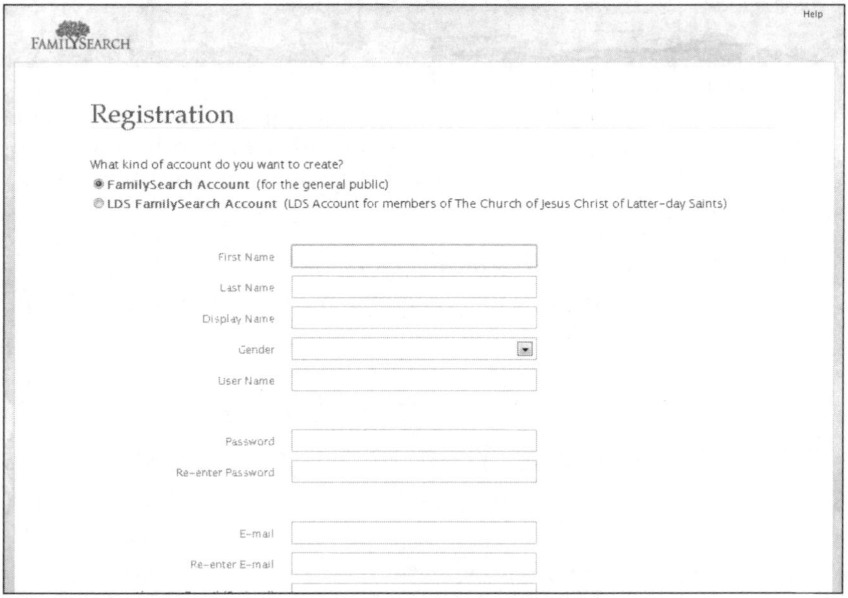

Registration

What kind of account do you want to create?

● FamilySearch Account (for the general public)
○ LDS FamilySearch Account (LDS Account for members of The Church of Jesus Christ of Latter-day Saints)

First Name	
Last Name	
Display Name	
Gender	
User Name	
Password	
Re-enter Password	
E-mail	
Re-enter E-mail	

Help

Figure 6-2

5. Check your e-mail account for the activation message.

6. In the activation message, click the Activate Account button. Your web browser launches and opens the account activation page.

7. Click the Continue button. This step returns you to the FamilySearch home page.

8. Click the Sign In link in the upper-right corner of the page. The Sign In page appears. (Refer to Figure 6-1.)

9. Enter your username and password in the appropriate fields, and click the Sign In button. After logging in successfully, you return to the FamilySearch home page, and your login display name appears in the upper-right corner of the page.

Searching Historical Records

From the FamilySearch records form, you can search all available databases in a single query. Multiple types of records are accessible via the form, including birth, marriage, death, probate, land, and military. Follow these steps to search all databases at one time:

1. Point your web browser to www.familysearch.org.

2. Enter the name of an ancestor into the First Names and Last Names fields, as shown in Figure 6-3.

Figure 6-3

3. If you want to match the name exactly, select the check boxes next to the First Names and Last Names fields.

You can use wildcards in your searches, if you want. See Chapter 5 for details.

4. Narrow your search by providing additional information about this person:

■ *Search by Life Events:* Click the Birth link, and enter the birthplace and birth year range, as shown in Figure 6-4. In the box that drops down, you can enter the exact birth date or enter an estimated year range.

Because record sets often contain imprecise dates, you may want to use the estimated year range first. If too many results are returned, you can then fine-tune your search by using the exact date. You can also enter additional life events by selecting the Marriage, Residence, Death, or Any links. To delete a line, simply click the Close (X) box in the upper-right corner of the Events box.

Figure 6-4

- *Search by Relationships:* Click the Spouse link, and then enter the spouse's first and last names. You can use wildcards in the names to assist your search.

- *Search by Batch Number:* If you know the *International Genealogical Index* (IGI) batch number, you can enter it by clicking the Batch Number link.

  The *IGI batch number* is used to find records that were entered into the index from the same record. You can use this number to find other names associated with the record that formed the batch. Normally, you can find a batch number by looking at a search result that comes from the IGI.

5. To limit the number of results, select the Match All Exactly check box.

6. Click the Search button to execute the search. The search results page appears, as shown in Figure 6-5. The results are divided into historical records at the top of the page and results from submitted pedigrees at the bottom.

Click to show preview of result.

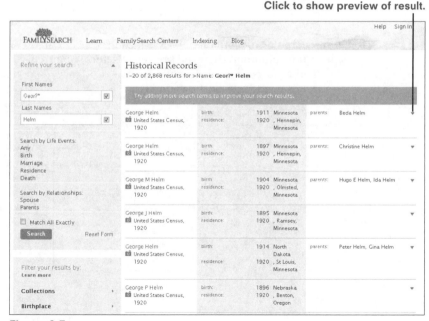

Figure 6-5

7. If you want to filter your results to a certain type of record, click a topic link in the lower-left corner of the page, under the Filter Your Results By heading, as shown in Figure 6-6.

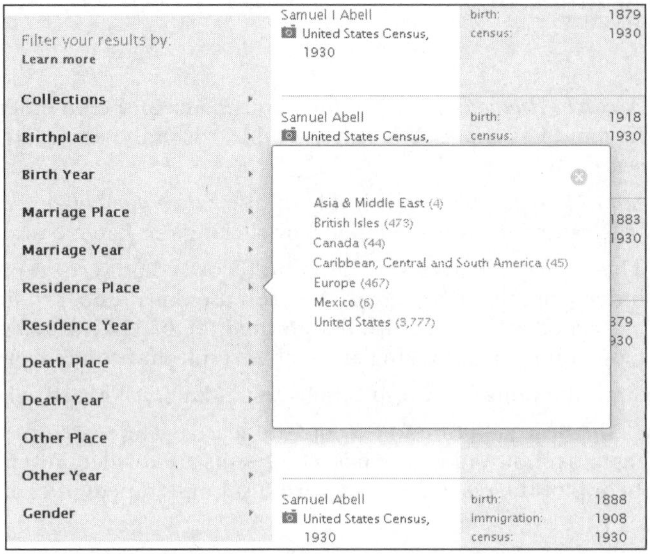

Figure 6-6

8. If the search result contains a preview, click the right arrow on the far right side of the column to show the preview. (Refer to Figure 6-5.) The preview shows other facts about the record, such as residence, date, relationship, gender, race, and age, as shown in Figure 6-7.

Figure 6-7

9. To view the record, click the name of the individual in the result. In our case, we clicked the name George Helm. The record page shown in Figure 6-8 appears with further information about the census record.

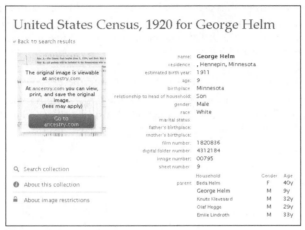

United States Census, 1920 for George Helm

◂ Back to search results

The original image is viewable at ancestry.com

At ancestry.com you can view, print, and save the original image. (fees may apply)

Go to ancestry.com

🔍 Search collection

ℹ️ About this collection

🔒 About image restrictions

name:	**George Helm**
residence:	, Hennepin, Minnesota
estimated birth year:	1911
age:	9
birthplace:	Minnesota
relationship to head of household:	Son
gender:	Male
race:	White
marital status:	
father's birthplace:	
mother's birthplace:	
film number:	1820836
digital folder number:	4312184
image number:	00795
sheet number:	9

Household	Gender	Age
parent: Beda Helm	F	40y
George Helm	M	9y
Knute Klevesard	M	32y
Olaf Hegge	M	29y
Emile Lindroth	M	33y

Figure 6-8

10. If the record contains a digitized image, click the Explore viewing options if you aren't logged in. If you're logged in, click the button leading to the external site.

An information box opens, showing options for viewing the digitized image. If the image is held on a subscription site, you may need to pay for a subscription.

11. When you click the link to the external site, a new browser window or tab may appear. After you finish at the external site, click the Close (X) box in the browser window or tab.

Browsing by Location

After you perform people searches, as in the preceding activity, you may want to survey the resources that are available for a particular location. It's useful to search by location to find other family members or to discover resources that might provide background information on the areas in which your ancestors lived. Follow these steps:

1. Scroll to the bottom of the FamilySearch home page.

2. In the Browse by Location section, click the USA, Canada, and Mexico link, as shown in Figure 6-9. You see a list of all historical record collections available for the United States, Canada, and Mexico.

Browse by Location

Africa
Asia and Middle East
Australia and New Zealand
Caribbean, Central and South America
Europe
Pacific Islands
USA, Canada, and Mexico

All Record Collections

Figure 6-9

3. You can narrow the list of collections in several ways:

   - *Type a search term:* In the Search box, type a location or subject that you want to search for. As you type in the Search box, the results on the right side of the page are automatically filtered. You can see an example of this filtering action in Figure 6-10, where we filtered on the search term *Illinois*.

   - *Select a filter:* To filter the records collections in a different way, click a filter on the left side of the page. For example, click the United States link in the Place section. The number of results on the right side of the page is reduced so that only those involving the United States are shown. You can click additional filters to narrow the results even further.

     To disable a filter, simply click the X to the right of the filter name.

   - *Limit search results to those with images*: Select the Show Only Collections with Images check box.

Enter location or subject to search.   Total collections available for location

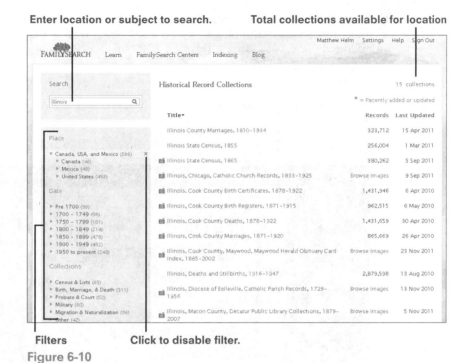

Filters   Click to disable filter.

Figure 6-10

4. To view the information page for the collection, click the collection name in the search results. For example, we clicked the link labeled Colorado State Census, 1885. Figure 6-11 shows the collection information page.

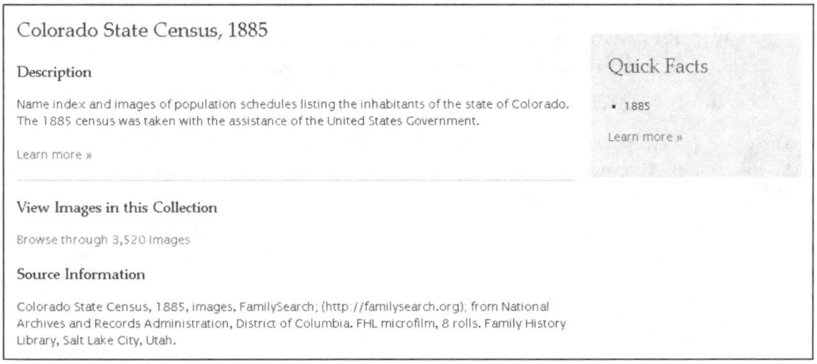

Figure 6-11

5. If the collection includes digital images, click the appropriate links to access those images. For example, to explore the Colorado State Census, 1885, we followed these links: Browse through 3,520 Images⇨Arapahoe⇨Denver⇨ Population. (See Figure 6-12.)

Tools to change the view   **Move to next page.**

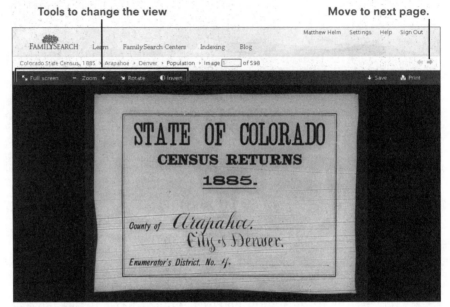

Figure 6-12

6. After you open an image in the collection, click the navigation elements (such as Zoom, Rotate, or Invert) to get a better look at the image.

7. To download a copy of the image, click Save. The image is saved to your default download folder in .jpg format.

8. If you want to print a copy of the image, click Print.

The printing screen for your browser opens. Because all browsers have their own ways of printing, you can use the options within your browser to produce the best possible print.

Discovering Family Trees

Before FamilySearch began digitizing records, it assembled a large collection of family trees in its Ancestral File collection, begun in 1979. The genealogies in this collection are arranged in pedigree charts for more than 40 million individuals. The information is based on user-submitted pedigree charts, family group sheets, and GEDCOM files.

 Because these pedigree charts, family group sheets, and GEDCOM files are user-submitted, most entries haven't been validated in any way. You should therefore use the entries as a guide to point you in the right direction — though you shouldn't necessarily take them as absolute truths. Be sure to verify any information from the Ancestral File, by validating it against original sources for accuracy. Follow these steps to search the family tree database:

1. On the FamilySearch home page, just under the "Discover Your Family History" heading, click the Trees link. The search page shown in Figure 6-13 appears.

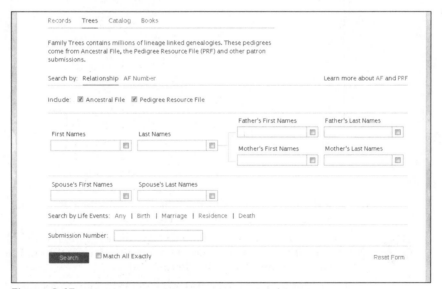

Figure 6-13

2. Fill out the fields for the ancestor you're researching. Remember to use wildcards in your search strings.

 One search choice, the AF (Ancestral File) Number field, lets you search based on a record number. This field is particularly useful in finding a person that you have previously discovered in the database.

3. Complete all relevant fields for your search, and click the Search button. The Tree search results page appears (see Figure 6-14).

The check boxes next to the names and places fields on the search page force the search to use an exact match. In the year adjustment fields on this page, you can instruct the search engine to look for a date that is a specific number of years on either side of a given date.

Current search criteria

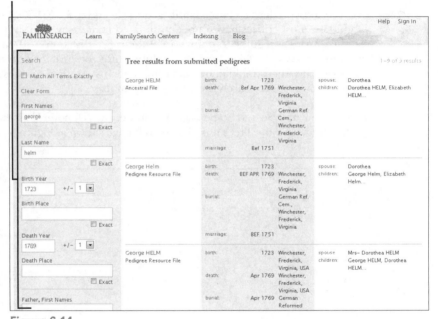

Figure 6-14

4. Click the name of an individual on the results page to see more information in the ancestral file, as shown in Figure 6-15.

The entry in the ancestral file may have links for the individual that tie to other relatives, such as spouse, father, mother, or children. Click the link to find information about the other individual.

5. If you want to print the record, click the Print button located in its upper-right corner.

You can use the AFN on the record to locate the entry quickly by using the Ancestral File Number search field on the search page.

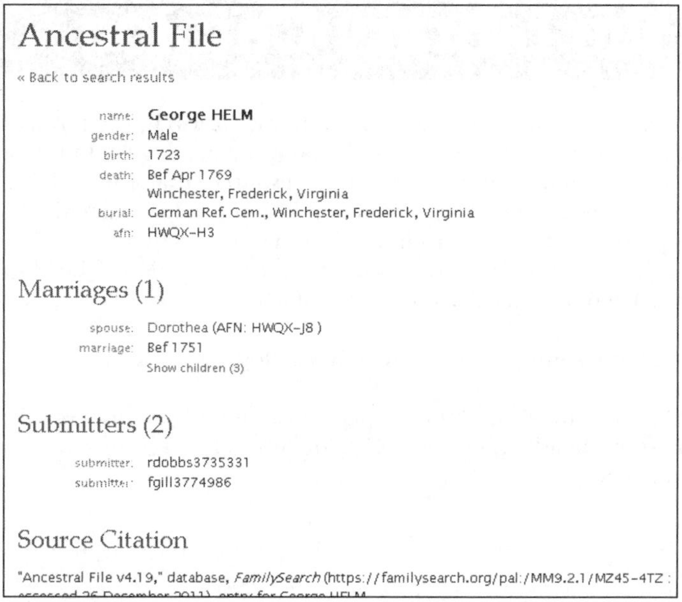

```
┌─────────────────────────────────────────────────────────┐
│  Ancestral File                                           │
│                                                           │
│  « Back to search results                                 │
│                                                           │
│              name:  George HELM                           │
│            gender:  Male                                  │
│             birth:  1723                                  │
│             death:  Bef Apr 1769                          │
│                     Winchester, Frederick, Virginia       │
│            burial:  German Ref. Cem., Winchester,         │
│                     Frederick, Virginia                   │
│               afn:  HWQX-H3                               │
│                                                           │
│  Marriages (1)                                            │
│                                                           │
│            spouse:  Dorothea (AFN: HWQX-J8 )              │
│          marriage:  Bef 1751                              │
│                     Show children (3)                     │
│                                                           │
│  Submitters (2)                                           │
│                                                           │
│         submitter:  rdobbs3735331                         │
│         submitter:  fgill3774986                          │
│                                                           │
│  Source Citation                                          │
│                                                           │
│  "Ancestral File v4.19," database, FamilySearch (https://familysearch.org/pal:/MM9.2.1/MZ45-4TZ : │
│  accessed 26 December 2011), entry for George HELM        │
└─────────────────────────────────────────────────────────┘
```

Figure 6-15

Resources available at FamilySearch

You can use a number of resources at FamilySearch:

- **Ancestral File**: A database with millions of names available in family group sheets and pedigree charts

- **Family History Library Catalog**: The library card catalog for the Family History Library in Salt Lake City

- **International Genealogical Index (IGI)**: A list of births and marriages of deceased individuals

- **Military Index**: A list of people killed in the Korean and Vietnam wars

- **Pedigree Resource File**: An index of user-contributed family trees

- **Social Security Death Index (SSDI)**: An index of persons for whom Social Security death claims were filed with the United States government

- **U.S. Census Records**: Indexes of the various U.S. censuses that are available to the public

- **Vital Records Index**: Index of birth, marriage, and death records

Using the Library Catalog

The FamilySearch website provides you with access to the library catalog of the Family History Library (FHL) — the largest genealogical library in the United States. You can use the catalog to find resources that are available only in book or microform format. A key collection of interest to family historians is the large number of family historians housed in the library. In all, the library contains more than 2.4 million rolls of microfilm, 727,000 microfiche, 356,000 books and serials, 4,500 periodicals, and 3,725 databases.

Follow these steps to search the FHL catalog:

1. On the FamilySearch home page, just under the "Discover Your Family History" heading, click the Catalog link. The page shown in Figure 6-16 appears.

Figure 6-16

2. From the Search drop-down menu, select the type of resource that you want to search on, such as Subjects.

3. Type your search term into the For field, and click the Search button. The Catalog search results page appears, as shown in Figure 6-17.

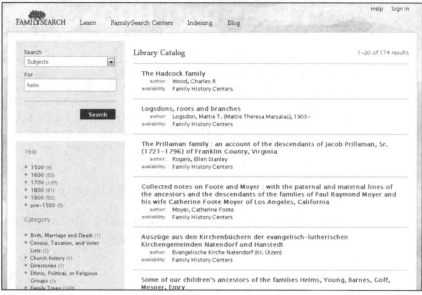

Figure 6-17

On the Catalog search results page, you can see the search terms you used in the left column. You can refine these terms at any time to begin a new search.

4. If you want to filter your results, use the filters on the left side of the page to filter by year, category, availability, or language.

5. Click a title to see more information about the work. The information specifies where the item is located and whether it can be sent to a local Family History Center.

Viewing Scanned Books

A project at the FamilySearch Labs (labs.familysearch.org) aims to place online a collection of family histories, county and local histories, how-to books, magazines, periodicals, medieval books, and gazetteers (geographical publications). These books come from the collections of the Family History Library, Allen County Public Library, Clayton Library Center for Genealogical Research at Houston Public Library (HPL), Mid-Continent Public Library, BYU Harold B. Lee Library, BYU Hawaii Joseph F. Smith Library, and the Church of Jesus Christ of Latter-day Saints Church History Library.

Follow these steps to search the collection of scanned books:

1. Set your web browser to books.familysearch.org. The site opens to the default simple search form, shown in Figure 6-18.

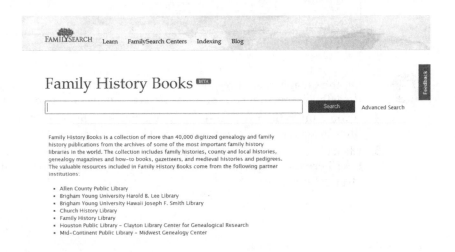

Figure 6-18

2. Click the Advanced Search link to the right of the Search button to open the Advanced Search form. (See Figure 6-19.)

Search restrictions

Search type   Search terms

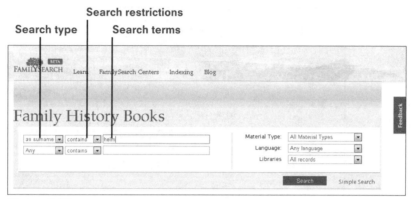

Figure 6-19

3. Underneath the heading "Family History Books," use the first row of fields to specify information about your search:
   - Click to open the first drop-down list, and select an option for the type of search you want to perform: Any (anywhere in the record), In the Title, As Author, As Surname, or Full Text.
   - Using the second drop-down list, you can restrict the search to look for a record that contains the search term, that's an exact word match, or that starts with the search term.
   - Type your search term or terms in the free-form text field, the last field on the first line.

4. On the right side of the page, select from these drop-down lists:
   - *Material Type:* Select the material type from the drop-down list. Eligible material types include books, periodicals/serials, and gazetteers.
   - *Language:* Select a language from the drop-down list. Available languages are English, French, German, Hungarian, and Spanish.
   - *Libraries:* If you want to limit the search to a book from a particular library, choose from the Libraries drop-down list: Family History Library, Allen County Public Library, BYU Harold B. Lee Library, Houston Public Library (Clayton Library Center), and Mid-Continent Public Library.

5. When you have selected all options, click the Search button. Figure 6-20 shows the result of a search on the surname *Helm* in any language or media.

6. If you receive too many results, you can use the filters in the left column.

   The search filters in the left column of the advanced form of the collections page include Language and Author/Creator. You have two additional options: suggested new searches by a certain author or creator and by a particular subject.

Figure 6-20

7. Click the title of a work to see the full text of the work. Figure 6-21 shows one such work.

Figure 6-21

The FamilySearch site uses a third-party product to display these works. In our case, the work was displayed in Internet Explorer and Mozilla Firefox but not in Google Chrome. Regardless of which browser you use, some works might take awhile to download.

Volunteering to Index

If you're interested in giving back to the family history community, one way is to join the worldwide FamilySearch Indexing Project, in which you select a record set that interests you and then participate as part of a team to index its records. The completed records are placed on the FamilySearch site for others to use for free. All indexing can be done from your home, whenever you have the time.

If you're interested in signing up for the indexing project, follow these steps:

1. On the FamilySearch home page, select the Indexing link at the top of the page.

2. On the right side of the Worldwide Indexing page, click the Get Started button.

3. On the Indexing page that appears, click the Download Now button to download the indexing program installation file.

4. Run (open) the installer to set up the indexing program on your computer.

5. Follow the prompts to install the program. On the installation screen, make sure the Run FamilySearch Indexing box is checked and click the Finish button.

6. Sign in using your FamilySearch account, as we explain in the earlier activity "Creating a FamilySearch Account." If you didn't create one, follow the instructions to create a new FamilySearch account by clicking the Register for a New Account button.

7. The indexing program asks you to choose a group for your profile. Select the Your Country radio button, United States of America from the Country drop-down list, and pick a state from the State or Province list. Then click OK.

8. Read the FamilySearch Indexing license agreement, click the I Agree button, and click OK.

9. You can click the Play Video button to view a video for new indexers. Otherwise, you can click Skip Video. The My Work portion of the indexing program loads on your screen.

10. To begin indexing, click the Download Batch button. A list of projects appears.

11. Click a project name, and then click the OK button. The record screen appears with some brief instructions.

12. Enter the appropriate information about the record in either the Table Entry or Form Entry portion of the indexing program (in the lower-left corner of the screen). The record is highlighted as you select elements to index. You can see an example in Figure 6-22.

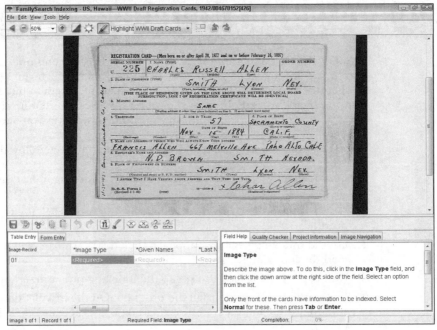

Figure 6-22

13. When you finish indexing the batch, follow the prompts to submit it.

Chapter 7

Gleaning Government Records

At some point in your life, you've surely been frustrated by being required to fill out long government forms simply to accomplish a simple task. Well, some of the time and labor that your ancestors also invested in completing those forms may pay off for you. One excellent source for family history evidence is found in government records that trace individuals throughout their lifecycles, from birth until death. These records also note significant life events such as marriages, divorces, land purchases, military service, and retirements.

Over the past decade, more and more government records have found their way online. In several cases, government agencies have realized the benefits of placing their records online for free use by family historians. In this chapter, we explore some of these sites and explain how to use them to find important documents related to your ancestors and their families.

tech to connect

activities

- Identifying sites that have government records
- Discovering the Civil War Soldiers and Sailors System
- Buying into the General Land Office
- Coming to Ellis Island
- Exploring the Online Public Access System at the National Archives

Identifying Sites with Government Records

One challenge you may face in searching government sites is determining which ones have records that are of use to family historians. Though you can find several "unofficial" sources of information about government records, such as bloggers and genealogically focused websites, you should investigate at least one official site — USA.gov.

Launched in September 2000 (and maintained by the United States General Services Administration's Office of Citizen Services and Innovative Technologies), USA.gov is the U.S. government's official *portal* (a site that points to information stored on several other sites) for locating government information. Because the site is supported by taxpayer money, feel free to use it to assist in your research efforts.

Follow these steps to locate sites with government records at USA.gov:

1. Go to the USA.gov home page at `www.usa.gov`, and click the Explore Topics button, shown in Figure 7-1.
2. Click the History, Arts, and Culture link in the middle column.
3. Select the History link.

Figure 7-1

4. Click the Family History and Genealogy link. The Family History and Genealogy page appears.

5. Click the link to a website that interests you.

Not every website listed on USA.gov is a government site. The USA.gov site may link to a nongovernment website that contains information of use to individuals who are looking for government information.

6. You can also find information via the USA.gov portal by using its search engine. From any page on the USA.gov site, locate the Search box at the top, type a search term such as *genealogy research*, and click the Search button (see Figure 7-2).

The USA.gov site uses the Bing search engine (`www.bing.com`) as its vertical index for government websites. A *vertical* index limits websites used by the search engine to only those that fit a specific subject matter.

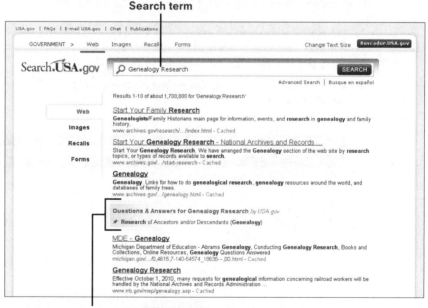

Figure 7-2

7. Click a result containing information that might assist your research.

Embedded in search results are links to other relevant content on USA. gov. When we searched for *genealogy research*, for example, a link to the site's Questions & Answers for Genealogy Research area appeared immediately after the third result (refer to Figure 7-2).

Discovering the Civil War Soldiers and Sailors System

One prolific source of military records in the United States comes from the American Civil War. The largest free collection of military records from that period is the Civil War Soldiers and Sailors System (CWSS). This joint project of the National Park Service (www.nps.gov), the Genealogical Society of Utah (www.gensocietyofutah.org), and the Federation of Genealogical Societies (www.fgs.org) contains an index of more than 6.3 million soldier records of both Union and Confederate soldiers and records from two prisoner of war (POW) camps. Also available at the site are regimental histories and descriptions of 384 battles.

Follow these steps to search for an ancestor at the CWSS site:

1. Set your web browser to www.itd.nps.gov/cwss to see the Civil War Soldiers and Sailors system home page.
2. Click the Soldiers link in the rightmost column.
3. On the Search by Soldier Name page, shown in Figure 7-3, enter the last name and first name on the form.

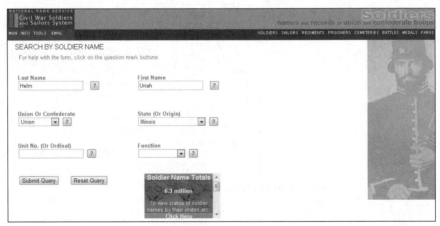

Figure 7-3

If you don't know of an American Civil War participant, you can use *Uriah Helm* to see what's available on the site.

4. Specify whether the participant was a Union or Confederate soldier by choosing ____ drop-down menu. In our case, Uriah Helm was a Un____

5. Fro____ , select the state in which your ancestor enl____

Un____ origin of the enlistment, or unless the par-tici____ ou can leave the State (or Origin) field alone. The____ only assumed to have enlisted from the state he____ ase — one of Matthew's ancestors, for example, live____ sted in a New Jersey regiment. You can leave the res____ you're sure of the unit number or type of mili-tar____

6. Aft____ , click the Submit Query button. Figure 7-4 dis-pla____ search for Uriah Helm.

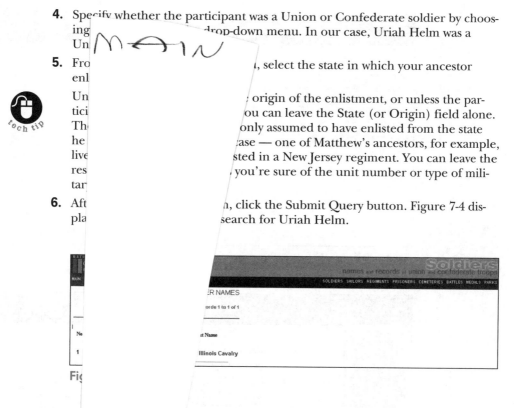

Fig____

7. Cl____ e participant to see more information about the indi-vidual. As you can see in Figure 7-5, the individual page shows the regiment name, company, rank on entering the regiment, rank on leaving the regi-ment, any alternative names used by the participant, notes, and the film number containing the source record. The image in the rightmost column is only a sample; it contains no information about the individual soldier.

8. Click the Back button in your web browser to return to the index page.

9. Click the regiment name to see its regimental history, as shown in Figure 7-6.

10. Click the name of a battle for more information about a particular engagement.

Figure 7-5

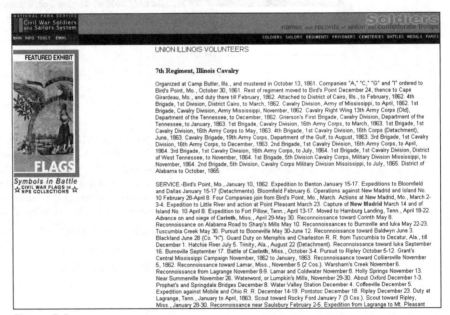

Figure 7-6

Buying Into the General Land Office

If your ancestors moved around a lot, you might discover information about them in land records. Although many available land records are stored at the local and state levels, some are maintained at the federal level — these records involve the sale or gifting of government-owned land. Sometimes, soldiers received bounty lands for their service in wars, and other pioneers gambled and bought government land to start fresh in new parts of the country.

The conveyance (the transfer into private hands) of federal lands is the responsibility of the General Land Office (GLO) within the Bureau of Land Management. The GLO website contains more than 5 million federal land title records that have been issued since 1820. The site also has images of *survey plats* (drawings of land boundaries) and *field notes* (narrative records of a survey) dating to 1810.

You can search for land records at the GLO website by following these steps:

1. Go to the GLO Records site at `www.glorecords.blm.gov`. This step opens the GLO home page.

2. In the green navigation bar near the top of the page, click the Search Documents link. The search form opens, as shown in Figure 7-7.

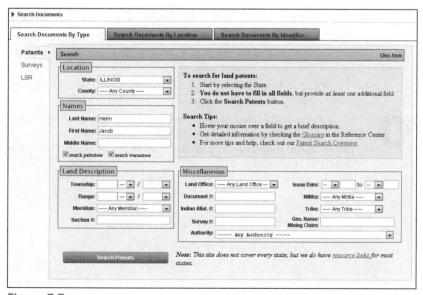

Figure 7-7

3. In the Location section of the search form, select a state.

Unless you know which county your ancestor lived in, don't worry about selecting one. This way, if your ancestor received land in more than one county, you see it in the results.

4. Fill in the Last Name and First Name fields for the ancestor you're researching. You can leave the Search Patentees and Search Warrantees check boxes selected so that the search includes both types of records.

5. Leave the rest of the fields alone, and click the Search Patents button at the bottom of the page. The Results List page appears, as shown in Figure 7-8.

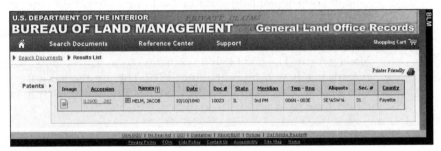

Figure 7-8

If you find a match, the Results List page shows you the name of the individual and facts about the land transaction, including its date, document number, state, meridian, township or range, aliquots, section number, and county.

6. Click the link in the Accession column to see additional details about the transaction. Figure 7-9 shows the Patent Details tab.

7. To see a digitized image of the record, such as the one shown in Figure 7-10, select the Patent Image tab.

8. Click the Related Documents tab to see other transactions that are geographically close to the property possessed by the individual.

The Related Documents page is useful for finding other individuals, and perhaps family members, who secured land near your ancestor. If plats are available on the website, you can also find them by using the Survey link on the Related Documents tab.

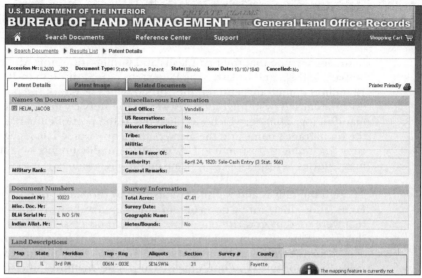

Figure 7-9

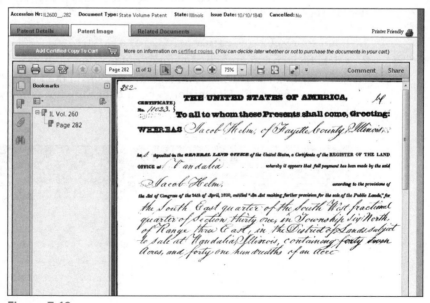

Figure 7-10

Coming to Ellis Island

Between the time that the first Ellis Island immigrant, Annie Moore, arrived on January 1, 1892, and its last, Arne Peterssen, passed through in 1954, more than 12 million immigrants entered the United States by way of the port. The key document used by immigration inspectors to interview immigrants was the ship's manifest log. The log, which was filled out at the port of embarkation, contained the immigrant's name and the answers to 29 questions. The log was also used to copy the immigrant's name to U.S. government documents — contrary to the many stories of inspectors Americanizing foreign names.

Though the Ellis Island website (sponsored by the Statue of Liberty–Ellis Island Foundation, Inc.) isn't a government-sanctioned website, it holds documents that were used by government inspectors while processing immigrants through the facility. Because the site has a fundraising goal, it has a heavy sales element. The records themselves are available for free, however, and after you get past the many items for sale (you don't have to purchase anything), the site holds information that is of value to family historians.

Before starting your first search, you need to register with the site. Follow these steps to register and then to search for a passenger:

1. Point your web browser to www.ellisisland.org.
2. Click the Sign In button in the upper-right corner of the page.
3. Click the link labeled Yes, I Am New to This Site in the right column, in the Are You New to This Site section. The membership form opens, as shown in Figure 7-11.

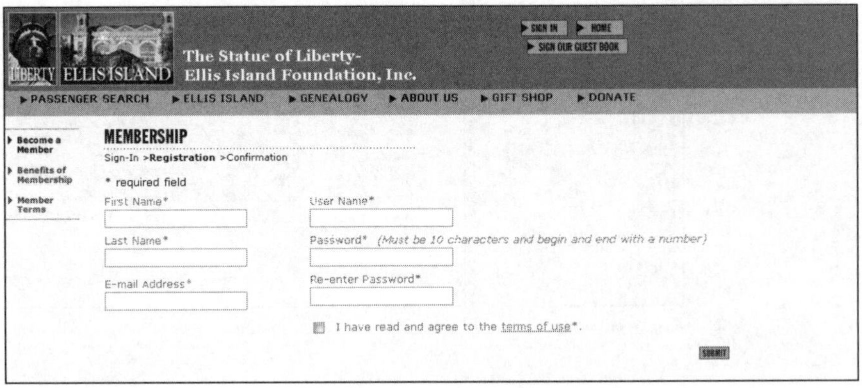

Figure 7-11

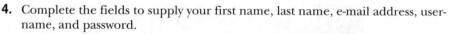
4. Complete the fields to supply your first name, last name, e-mail address, user-name, and password.

Your password must consist of ten characters and begin and end with numbers. To verify your password, you must enter it twice.

5. Select the check box verifying that you have read and have agreed to the terms of use. Then click the Submit button. The Registration Confirmation screen appears. You aren't required to become a contributing member of the foundation.

6. Click the Passenger Search link in the blue navigation bar near the top of the page.

7. In the search form, type the first and last names of the passenger.

8. If you know the year of birth, enter it in the Approximate Year of Birth field. Use the drop-down menu next to the field to set a year range for the date.

Set the year of birth to the *+ or –5 year* option, even if you know the year of birth from another source. Often, birth dates on passenger manifests weren't exact, and expanding the search criteria can help return better results.

9. Select a gender from the drop-down menu. A completed search form is shown in Figure 7-12.

Figure 7-12

10. Click the Start Search button. The search results page appears, as shown in Figure 7-13, listing the passenger's name, residence, year of arrival, and age on arrival, and links to further information.

11. Click the View link in the Passenger Record column. The passenger record (which is a fancy way to display information from the foundation indexes) includes the passenger's name, last residence, date of arrival, age at arrival, ship of travel, port of departure, and manifest line number.

The Ellis Island site gives you the option to order a certificate, if you want.

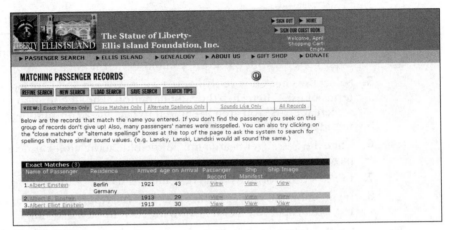

Figure 7-13

12. At the top of the page, select the Original Ship Manifest link. The page then shows a digitized copy of the ship manifest, which is more valuable than the passenger record, which is simply a transcription of this record.

13. Select the Click to Enlarge Manifest link in the rightmost column of the manifest image window.

The image of the manifest may appear in a new browser window. If so, maximize the browser to see the full view of the image, as shown in Figure 7-14. You may also find that some manifests are two pages long. (The second page contains valuable information, not including the name of the passenger.) The index finds the second page first. In this case, navigate to the previous page to see the name by clicking the Previous link next to the image.

14. Click the Close Window button to remove the extra browser window.

15. Click the Ship link near the top of the page. If a picture and basic information about the ship are available, they're displayed on the page, as shown in Figure 7-15.

16. Click the View Annotations link near the top of the page to see additional information about your ancestor.

Registered members of the site can post annotations to the records with further information about the individual. Because the annotations are contributed by users, you must verify any information that's presented on the Annotations page.

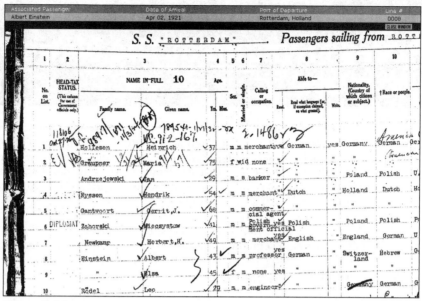

Figure 7-14

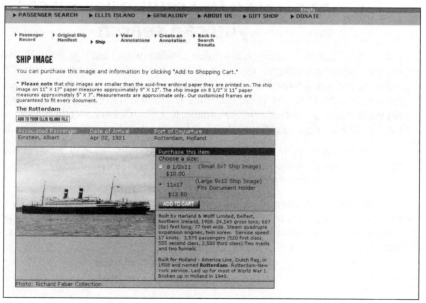

Figure 7-15

Exploring the Online Public Access System at the National Archives

The United States National Archives and Records Administration (NARA) preserves the records of the United States federal government. This agency has traditionally preserved important records by microfilming them and making the microfilms available for purchase. However, over the past few years, the Archives has worked to place more resources online, in addition to working with digitization partners such as Ancestry.com.

You can use the Online Public Access (OPA) tool at the National Archives website to search several online resources at the same time, including its Archival Research Catalog, Access to Archival Databases, Archives.gov website, and Electronic Records Archive.

Exploring the online resources you can search

The *Archival Research Catalog* is the online catalog of the holdings of the National Archives. The catalog includes the holdings of the Washington, D.C.–area Archives facilities, regional archives, and presidential libraries. More than 6 billion records are contained within the catalog. In addition to descriptions of materials held within the archives, more than 153,000 digitized images are included in the catalog. Not all Archives collections are described in the catalog. The catalog was about 68 percent complete when we wrote this book.

You use the *Access to Archival Databases* to access online a small group of historical databases maintained by the National Archives. The Archives selected 475 databases to place online and continues to add to them.

The collection of documents in the *Electronic Records Archive* were originally created electronically. Though this area gives you access to the full text of documents that have been determined to be free of any access restrictions, not all electronic documents under NARA have been reviewed and released to the public.

Follow these steps to search the OPA system at the National Archives site:

1. Point your web browser to the `www.archives.gov` home page.
2. Click the Research Our Records button in the upper-left corner of the page.
3. In the Search Online section, click the Try Our New Online Public Access System link.
4. Click the Advanced Search link underneath the Search Online Public Access field. This step opens the advanced search form within the OPA system, as shown in Figure 7-16.

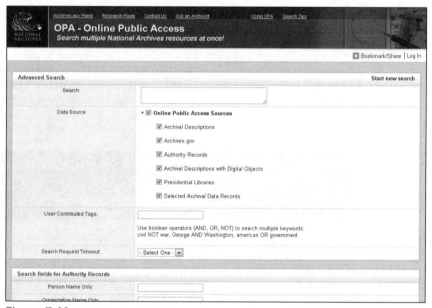

Figure 7-16

5. Type the subject of your search in the Search field.
6. Configure the remaining Advanced Search options in these sections of the search form:

   ■ *Data Source:* You can control the types of resources that the search engine uses by deselecting check boxes in the Data Source section. If you don't want to search presidential libraries, for example, simply deselect the check box.

- *User Contributed Tags:* Users can contribute their own tags to the records held within OPA. If you want to search them, fill in the User Contributed Tags field. Not much of the content has user-contributed tags, so use this field only when you know that someone has tagged a particular entry you're looking for.

- *Search Request Timeout:* Because the search engine is looking at several systems, searches can take some time. You can control the length of time the search engine takes by setting the Search Request Timeout value. Use this option only when your searches are taking a very long time and affecting your ability to search. For example, use this setting whenever your web browser times out after a search exceeds the time limit.

7. Use the options in the Search Fields for Authority Records section and the Search Fields for Archival Descriptions section only when you're looking for a particular record set.

8. Click the Search button at the bottom of the form to begin the search. The search results page appears, looking similar to the one shown in Figure 7-17. The results are grouped by holding type, which includes these common types: online, description only, Archives.gov results, presidential libraries, and NARA authority records.

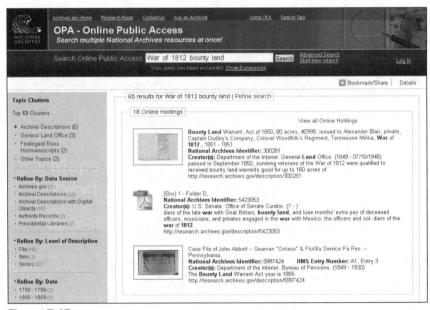

Figure 7-17

9. If you receive too many results, filter them by clicking criteria in the leftmost column (in blue), such as Data Source, Level of Description, Date, Type of Archival Materials, File Format, or Location.

10. Click the title of the resource to see additional information.

Figure 7-18 shows the result of clicking a resource to see additional information about an online holding. The left column describes the records hierarchy — that is, how you would find the item cataloged within the archives. In the section underneath it, you can add a user-contributed tag to the item, such as the person's name on the document. In the right column is a digital image of the document (only if it pertains to online holdings). Beneath the image is an identifier number and information about the creator of the document.

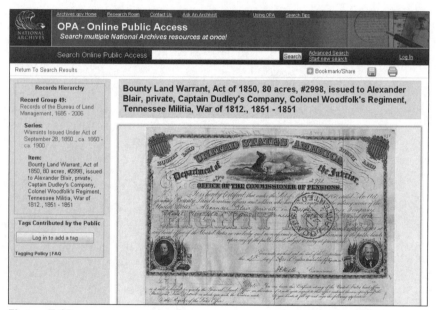

Figure 7-18

11. At the bottom of the page, click the Additional Information about This Item link to see more details about the item, including the scope and context of the record set, NARA control numbers and identifiers (useful if you need to contact NARA about the record), and the physical location of the record.

Chapter 8

Using Geographic Records and Maps

Even if your family has lived in the same town or county for generations, your genealogy research will eventually lead you to locate records in another place. Some of these records are geography-based (such as land records), and others, though they aren't inherently geographical, reflect information about life events that have taken place in other locations. In some situations, you may need information about a general location to make sense of a specific event that occurred there and in which your ancestor participated. This need can help you determine your next step in researching or finding where that relative moved after the event or as a result of it.

Additionally, you may want to visit locations where significant events happened in your ancestor's life. For example, you may want to see your great-grandfather's homestead or pay your respects at his grave. *Gazetteers* (geographical dictionaries) and maps can help you identify places and locate them.

activities

tech to connect

- Searching for geographic-based records
- Using a current online map
- Finding a location with a gazetteer
- Seeing the world through Google Earth
- Distinguishing landforms with topographic maps
- Downloading a map from the U.S. Geological Survey

Searching for Geography-Based Records

A variety of websites contain geography-based information, including online information about records related to a particular town, county, state, or country or to another type of locality. You can find sites devoted to cemeteries in specific counties, sites that contain land records sorted by county or state, and sites that let you search historical city directories. If you're looking for records stored in a local or county courthouse, for example, you may not be able to find a site related to only that courthouse.

Because many records are geography-based and are stored on various websites, it's a good idea to search using the advanced features of search engines. Suppose that you're looking for your great-great-grandfather's grave site. You know his name, and all the information that you've found or heard about so far indicates that he died in a particular state.

Follow these steps to search for geography-based information:

1. Point your browser to the popular Google search engine at www.google.com. (Though we use Google in our example, feel free to use your favorite search engine.)

2. In the Search field, enter search terms that are as specific as possible. For example, if you're looking for a grave site, type your ancestor's first and last names in quotation marks, type the word *grave*, and type the name of the state, as shown in this example: *"Harris Sanders" grave Mississippi*.

   By enclosing the first and last name in quotation marks, you tell the search engine to use a *proximity* search, in which it looks for the two names as one phrase.

3. Click the Google Search button, underneath the main Search field. Google processes your search terms and returns its results. You can see the results from the sample search in Figure 8-1.

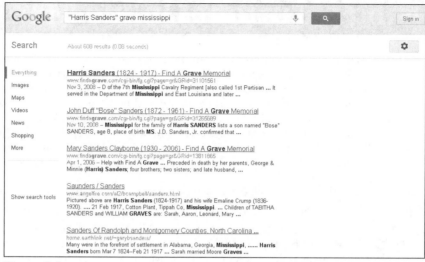

Figure 8-1

4. Scroll the list of results to see whether any of them looks promising. If one (or more) does, click the link to that site to see what it has to offer.

5. If none of the results appears relevant to your ancestor, add or delete search terms and try again.

    Adjust your search terms based on the results of your first search. If the search returned too many results (thousands or hundreds of thousands, for example), refine the search terms by adding more specific information, such as additional names (middle name of ancestor, name of spouse, or nickname) or dates (date of birth or year of death, for example). If only a few results were returned in the first search, expand it by removing a term, such as the state name. Or modify your search by deleting the name of the state and adding dates.

6. Repeat Steps 2 through 5 as needed.

Using a Current Online Map

Maps help you achieve two main tasks in your family history research: See where your ancestors were located over time (and plot their paths, in some cases), and find the current locations of your ancestors' life events so that you can visit those spots. There are several online mapping sites including Google Maps (maps. google.com) and Yahoo! Maps (maps.yahoo.com). While most of the online mapping sites have the same basic functionality, we picked MapQuest to use as an example here. To search for a geographical location on a current map, follow these steps:

1. Using your favorite web browser, head to MapQuest at www.mapquest.com.

2. In the Search For field, type the location you're looking for.

   You include the name of a geographical location, plus its city and state, or identify only the city and state. Separating the place, city, and state by commas is helpful. For example, when we looked for the cemetery where one of our ancestors is buried, we typed *2261 County Road 700, Blue Mountain, Mississippi.*

3. Click the Get Map button. As you can see in Figure 8-2, the map of Blue Mountain, Mississippi, is generated with a pushpin icon marking the location of the cemetery.

Figure 8-2

4. Using the navigation icons on the right side of the screen, zoom in or out or move the view of the location by using the compass.

If you're planning to visit the location personally, find driving directions by clicking the Get Directions button under the Search For field in the upper-left corner. Enter the starting location of your journey in the topmost field, labeled A. The location you searched for in Steps 1–3 appears in the field labeled B. Click the Get Directions button.

Finding a Location with a Gazetteer

The geographical dictionary known as a *gazetteer* provides information about physical locations. Most current gazetteers provide location names, regional data (if available), and latitude and longitude.

Gazetteers are helpful in family history research because they give you additional information about locations that can help you determine whether commonly named places are the ones you're looking for. After you pinpoint exactly where an ancestor lived, you can determine where else to look for records.

Follow these steps to find a location with a gazetteer:

1. Point your web browser to the U.S. Geological Survey's Geographic Names Information System (GNIS) at `http://geonames.usgs.gov/pls/gnispublic`. The search form for the United States and its territories appears.

2. In the Feature Name field, enter the name of the place you're looking for. To find information about Blue Mountain, Mississippi, for example, enter **Blue Mountain** in the Feature Name field, as shown in Figure 8-3.

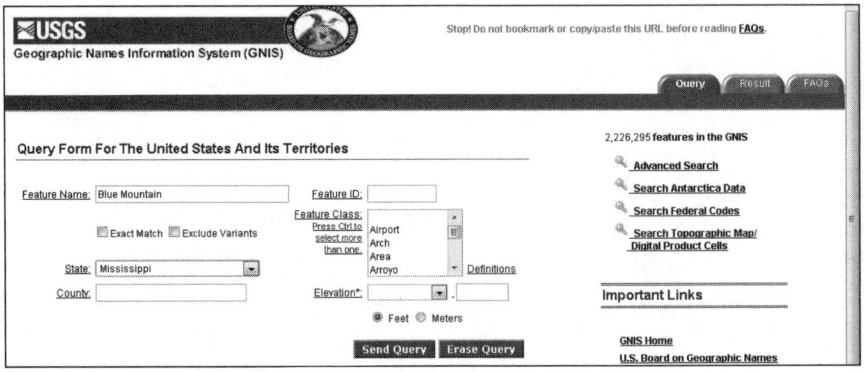

Figure 8-3

3. Skip the Feature ID field. GNIS assigns feature ID numbers to places, but you don't know the number the first time you look for a place using the GNIS site.

4. In the Feature Class area, scroll the list to select the type of location you're searching. In the Blue Mountain example, we don't select a feature class,

which should yield results that include any type of feature class with *Blue Mountain* in its name.

To select more than one feature class, press the Ctrl key on your keyboard as you click each one.

5. If you want to restrict the search by exact matches only or to exclude certain types of locations, select the check box next to either of the options Exact Match or Exclude Variant.

6. If you know the name of the state where the location is, enter it in the State field. We entered **Mississippi** in the example.

7. If you know the name of the county where the location is, enter it in the County field.

8. Leave the Elevation field blank.

Including the elevation is one way to restrict the results when searching on a feature or location. After you've used GNIS a few times and you're more proficient in how it works, you may choose to include elevation. It isn't necessary the first time, however.

9. Review your search terms and click the Send Query button.

10. Review the list of results and click any that match the type of location you're looking for. The results of a search on Blue Mountain, Mississippi, are shown in Figure 8-4. We clicked the top result for Blue Mountain (shown as the Populated Place in the Class column) to generate a feature detail report with information about the town.

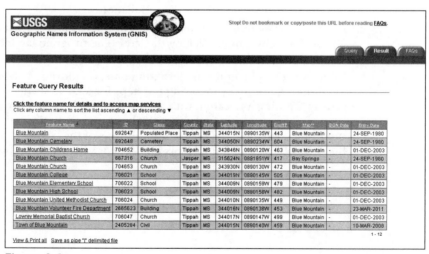

Figure 8-4

Seeing the World through Google Earth

The Internet has done wonders for mapping capabilities. No longer do you have to rely on only a one-perspective, two-dimensional map to convey a location. Technology lets you use multiple maps simultaneously — by overlaying details whether they relate changes in space or time — so that you can paint a big picture of your ancestral homelands.

The downloadable program Google Earth combines Google searches with geographic information. It presents the earth as a graphical globe on which you can map a place name or a latitudinal-longitudinal coordinate. Follow these steps to download Google Earth and use it to map a location:

1. Open your favorite web browser and go to Google Earth at `www.google.com/earth/index.html`.

2. Click the button labeled Download Google Earth.

3. Read the agreement. Then select whether to also download the Google Chrome web browser and make it your default browser by selecting the check boxes next to those options.

4. Click the Agree and Download button. The download begins automatically. Depending on your operating system, you may have to give Google Earth permission to download and run the installation.

5. After the installation is complete, go to your computer's desktop and open Google Earth by double-clicking the icon. The program launches and shows the earth as it looks from space, as shown in Figure 8-5.

6. In the Search field, enter the location name, or address, or latitude and longitude (as found by following the steps for a GNIS search in the earlier activity "Finding a Location with a Gazetteer"). Then click the Search button. Google Earth zooms in and shows the location with a crosshair on the precise spot. In the example, we entered the address of the cemetery at 2261 County Road 700, Blue Mountain, Mississippi. The results are shown in Figure 8-6.

Search field

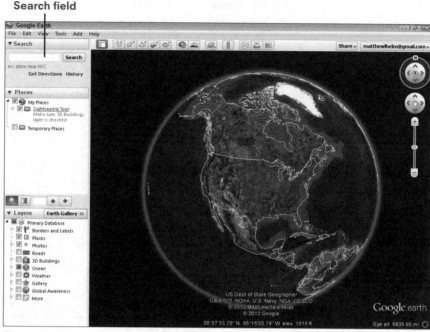

Figure 8-5

7. Click the Add Placement icon (the yellow pushpin) in the row along the top
    of the right pane. This step opens the New Placemark dialog box (shown in
    Figure 8-7) so that you can provide specific information about this location.
    The pushpin marks the location on the map so that it's easier to see. Click OK
    to close the dialog box.

8. Select check boxes in the Layers section, in the lower-left corner of the
    screen, to overlay the base map and placemark with various layers. Free
    Rumsey historical maps can sometimes overlay the area to show you what the
    land looked like in the early to mid-1800s.

9. In some cases, you may be able to click the Show Historical Imagery icon
    (the clock) in the bar along the top of the right pane to see the land at
    specific periods. For example, we can see the land for the cemetery in Blue
    Mountain, Mississippi, at periods between 1996 and 2007. To see different
    periods, you use the slider on the timeline tool that is then displayed.

Add Placemark   Show Historical Imagery

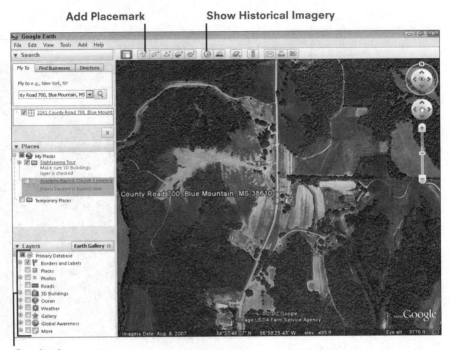

Overlay base map

Figure 8-6

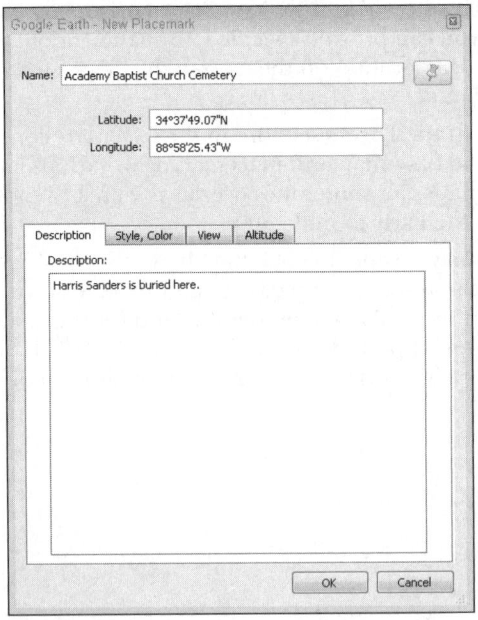

Figure 8-7

Distinguishing Landforms with Topographic Maps

A helpful type of map in family history research is the *topographic* map, which shows you feature types such as ridges, mountains, and creeks. The topographic map contains information about land features — whether natural or manmade, which can help you understand the geographic conditions in which your ancestors lived. Topographic maps are also helpful when you do on-site research such as trying to locate a cemetery. The maps typically contain information that is not found on a traditional atlas or highway map. To check out topographical maps at the U.S. Geological Survey (USGS) National Map site, follow these steps:

1. Go to The National Map website at `http://nationalmap.gov`.

2. In the leftmost column, click the Historical Topographic Map Collection link. The Historical Topographic Maps — Preserving the Past page opens.

   The USGS site offers a couple of ways to search its digitized maps that are available for viewing and downloading: Complete a search by using elements of the map name and metadata, or look for available maps using a map-based tool. (Map *metadata* is information that describes the map and helps you efficiently search for a particular one.)

3. In the Find My Map section (in the text section in the middle column), click the Historical Topographic Map Collection Search link. This step opens the search form shown in Figure 8-8.

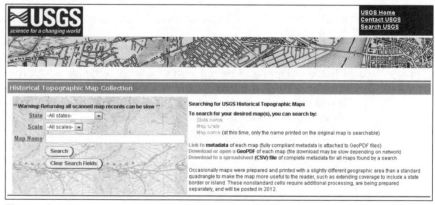

Figure 8-8

4. Select a state from the drop-down menu, type the specific location name in the Map Name field, and click the Search button. If you search by state alone, a list is generated of all available maps for that region. For example, because the site offers no historical topographic maps for Mississippi (yet), we searched for all maps identified as Indian territory. The results are shown in Figure 8-9.

The USGS digital collection of historical maps is only now getting underway, so you may not yet find a map specifically for the location you're researching. However, the collection is growing quickly, so check back often.

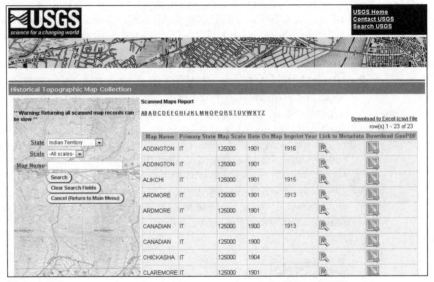

Figure 8-9

5. Click the paper-and-pencil icon to link to metadata about the map, or click the map-with-arrow icon to download a copy of the map in .pdf format. If you choose the latter option, follow the prompts from your computer to either open or save the file.

Downloading a Map from the U.S. Geological Survey

As you can discover in the preceding activity, the U.S. Geological Survey (USGS) has an assortment of maps of the United States and Canada that can be useful — and fun and interesting — in your genealogical research. Follow these steps to find and download many *additional* types of maps at USGS:

1. Go to The National Map website at `http://nationalmap.gov`.
2. In the left pane, click the Historical Topographic Map Collection link. (This step initially opens the same page as in the preceding activity.)
3. Click the USGS Store: Map Locator and Downloader link in the Find My Map section in the middle column. This step opens the Map Locator & Downloader page, shown in Figure 8-10.

Navigation tools

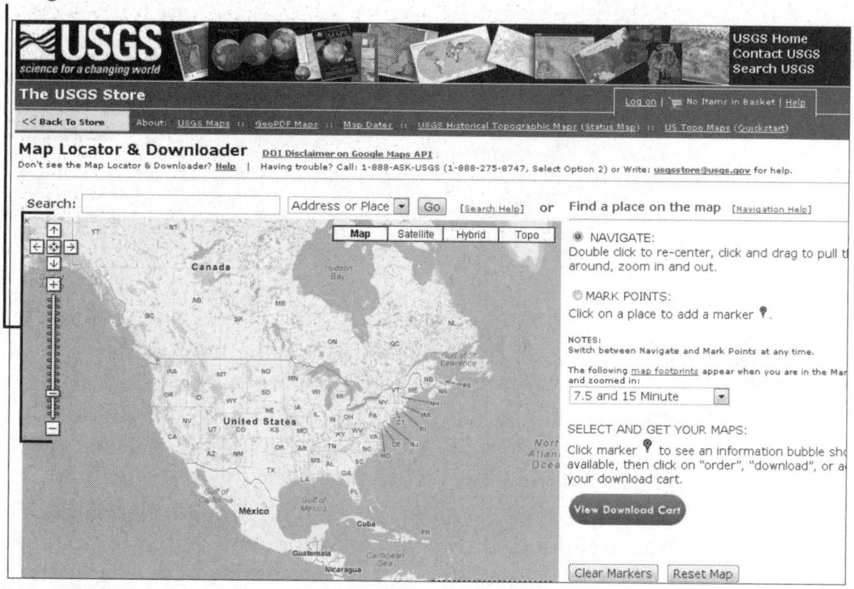

Figure 8-10

4. Type the location name in the Search field, and click Go to navigate to that location on the map. We're looking for maps that show Blue Mountain, Mississippi, as in earlier activities in this chapter, so we typed this location in the Search field and clicked Go. On the results page, a red balloon marker appears, marking the location on a map.

5. Use the navigation tools on the left side of the screen to center and zoom to see different perspectives of the map.

6. You can click the four options in the upper-right corner of the map to see it in different formats: Map, Satellite, Hybrid, or Topo.

The Hybrid map type shows the satellite image overlaid with data from the general map, such as roads, labels, and points of interest. The educational Topo option lets you see the topographic map of the area, which shows various landforms such as rivers, mountains, and lowlands. See Figure 8-11 for an example of the topographic map of Blue Mountain.

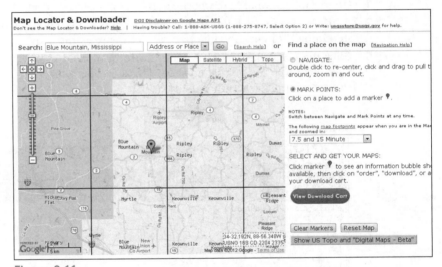

Figure 8-11

7. Click the red balloon marker to see whether maps are available for download or purchase. A menu of options pops up.

8. Click the file-size link in the Download column to download a copy of the map in .pdf format. For example, to download a copy of the Blue Mountain map, we clicked the 4.8 MB link at the top of the column.

9. Follow the download instructions and prompts to open or save the file on your computer. If you plan to include this map in your genealogical database for reference, save it to an easily accessible folder on your computer.

10. To have the USGS send you a paper copy of the map, if one is available, click the map name link in the Buy column of the options menu. (Refer to Step 7.) Otherwise, click to close the menu, and then you can change the location in the Search field and look at maps of another place or close your browser if you're finished working with maps.

Chapter 9

Mapping Land Records at HistoryGeo.com

T he new subscription website HistoryGeo.com lets you overlay maps and data to create a big-picture map of your ancestors' residences in the United States. The maps are handy for showing migration patterns, the proximity of residences or graves, and general location-based information. The site also offers the potential to interact with other researchers and to share map-based resources and information.

tech to connect

activities

- Registering for a free account
- Learning about the HistoryGeo Map Viewer
- Updating your profile
- Working with other researchers

Registering for a Free Account at HistoryGeo.com

To use the resources at HistoryGeo.com, you must first have an account. It's easy, and it's free. Here's how to register:

1. Using your favorite web browser, go to www.historygeo.com.
2. Click the Register Your Free Account link.
3. On the Registration page, type your e-mail address in the E-Mail field.
4. Enter a password, and type it again in the Confirm Password field.
5. Type your first name in the First Name field, enter your middle name or initial in the Middle field (optional), and type your last name in the Last Name field.
6. In the Home Town/State field, enter the name of the town and state where you live, if you want.

Checking system requirements

Though the innovative HistoryGeo.com site is fun and interesting to use, it has specific hardware and software requirements. If your computer is older, you may not be able to access the site or use it effectively. To avoid pitfalls and frustrations, follow these steps to check out the HistoryGeo requirements and evaluate your computer's compatibility:

1. Click the Learn link. It's on the blue navigation bar near the top of the page. This step opens the HistoryGeo KnowledgeBase, where you can find questions and answers about the site and its resources.

2. Scroll down the page and click the System Requirements link.

3. To see quickly whether your computer meets the system requirements, click the Run These Tests link.

Most likely, you know what type of computer and operating system you have (Mac versus Windows). However, you may need to look in your computer's list of programs or applications to see whether you have the required software. Additionally, you may need to open a software application and click its Help link (usually in the upper-right corner) to determine which version your computer has.

Choosing a strong password

When you create a password at an online site, pick a word or a name that you can remember easily but not one that's closely associated with you, which other people can guess. Many sites recommend that you create a *strong* password — one that combines uppercase and lowercase letters, numbers, and special characters, such as asterisks, exclamation points, or ampersands.

7. Click the Gender radio button that applies to you.

8. Click the Terms of Use link, and review the terms. If you agree to them, select the check box labeled I Agree to the Terms of Use.

9. Click the Register button. This step generates your membership profile and opens your member page. You can see our new membership page in Figure 9-1.

Figure 9-1

Learning about the HistoryGeo Map Viewer

To view and manipulate maps on the HistoryGeo website, you use its Map Viewer tool. The base registration lets you open and use the viewer with free maps, but you must have a paid subscription to use the majority of the maps. In this activity, we give you an overview of the viewer, though your viewing capability and activity on the site may be limited based on the free registration status, which we use in this step list (and which we show you how to set up in an earlier activity in this chapter).

Follow these steps to use the HistoryGeo Map Viewer:

1. If you aren't already signed in to your HistoryGeo account from the previous activity, sign in now.
2. Click the Launch Map Viewer link on the blue navigation bar. The viewer launches, displaying a map of the United States, as shown in Figure 9-2.

   Use the zoom and arrow navigation tools on the left side of the viewer to move the map around and zoom in or out, depending on the location you want to view. Depending on the type of mouse or touchpad you use, you may be able to drag and zoom without using the icons on the web page.
3. Click the View Map List button at the top of the viewer (next to the logo). The Map Chooser dialog box opens, as shown in Figure 9-3.
4. Select values in the Map Chooser, including the State and Counties menus. As you select values, the list auto-populates.
5. Highlight the map collection in the Map Chooser, and click the Open button to the right of it. The map displays in the viewer. If you have a subscription to add maps to your collection for use with the viewer, you can select maps to view and manipulate.
6. Using the Camera icon in the navigation tools, you can mark a specific location on a map to include in your list of snapshots. (A snapshot is simply a way to place a bookmark on a map.) Zoom in on the location, and click the Camera icon. A dialog box opens, where you can add information about the location. Click OK when you're finished.
7. If you want to add a customized marker to your map, zoom in to the location on the map where you want to post additional information, click the pushpin icon, and click the location on the map. A dialog box opens, in which you can add explanations and photos. Click the Save button when you're finished.
8. When you finish using the HistoryGeo Viewer, close it by clicking the Close Viewer button in the upper-right corner of the screen. This step returns you to the main HistoryGeo web page, where you can access your general member page and the free content on the site.

Zoom In

Take Snapshot of Current View

Click to close viewer.

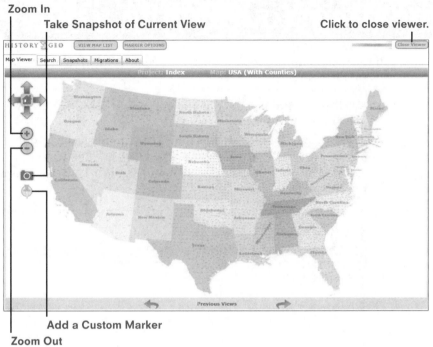

Add a Custom Marker

Zoom Out

Figure 9-2

Figure 9-3

Updating Your Profile

If you want to update the information in your HistoryGeo profile, sign in and follow these steps:

1. Click the My Profile button in the upper-right corner of the screen, under the Logged In As line.

2. Click the Edit Profile Info link under your profile image and the About Me section of your member profile page. (Refer to Figure 9-1.)

3. On the Edit Your Profile page, shown in Figure 9-4, update your information.

Figure 9-4

In the first free-form text field on the Edit Your Profile page, provide information about yourself and your research interests. Identify your hometown and provide your date of birth, and then choose whether to display this information. You can even designate your gender or change it, if needed. Finally, indicate whether you want your group memberships displayed on your profile page for others to see.

4. When you finish updating your profile information, click the Save Profile button.

Working with Other Researchers

After you start working with the maps at HistoryGeo.com, you may want to collaborate with other researchers. Finding collaborators is as simple as searching for them. Sign in and follow these steps:

1. Click the My Profile button in the upper-right corner of the screen, underneath the Logged In As line.
2. Click either the Friends link or the Groups link.
3. In the field labeled Find Existing Member or Find Existing Groups, type a location name, keyword, or surname related to your research interests. See Figure 9-5 for an example.

Figure 9-5

4. Click the Search button.
5. Scroll the results, and click on any that interest you. Figure 9-6 shows the results of our sample search for groups related to Grayson County, Texas.
6. If your research interests seem to fit with those of the person or group and you want to collaborate, click either the Send a Friend Request button or the Join the Group button.

Figure 9-6

Chapter 10

Looking at Specialized Online Collections

In earlier chapters of this book, we explore a couple of genealogy websites that can be helpful in your research. But smaller, lesser-known sites have helpful information and records too. In fact, some smaller sites have online record sets of limited size, specialize in a particular type of record (such as military and census records) or cover certain periods. Though these sites may not have the same level of coverage as the Ancestry.com site, they often have record sets that aren't available on larger sites. Some of these smaller sites might contain a record or two that you haven't yet discovered, which can fill in a gap in your research.

tech 2 connect

activities

- Registering at Fold3
- Searching Fold3 for military records
- Viewing images on Fold3
- Sharing records at Fold3
- Reviewing Archives.com

Registering at Fold3

Fold3 (formerly Footnote.com) specializes in military records, although it also has homestead records, city directories, passport applications, and census records. The name of the site comes from the traditional flag-folding ceremony, where the third fold of the flag symbolizes the remembrance of veterans who have served in defense of the country. The site, owned by Ancestry.com, contains more than 85 million images and more than 100 million memorial pages. (A *memorial* page is based on a particular individual found in a record set.) The site contains records from these conflicts: American Revolution, War of 1812, Mexican-American War, early Indian Wars, American Civil War, World War I, World War II, and Vietnam War.

Follow these steps to sign up at Fold3:

1. Set your web browser to www.fold3.com.
2. Click the 7-Day Free Trial Access Everything button in the upper-right corner of the page.
3. Click the orange Start Free Trial button in the left column. The Create Your Fold3 Profile page appears, as shown in Figure 10-1.

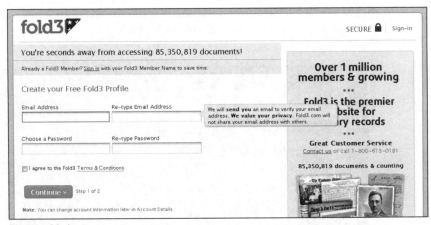

Figure 10-1

4. Fill out the e-mail address and password fields, and select the check box labeled I Agree to the Fold3 Terms and Conditions. Then click the Continue button.

Be sure to click the Terms & Conditions link and read the Fold3 Terms of Use page so that you understand what you can and cannot do with the material on the Fold3 site. The page also specifies what the site does with the information you provide as you use the site.

5. Fill out the payment information, including cardholder name, card number, expiration date, billing zip code, country, and phone number.

Unfortunately, Fold3 requires credit card information in order to initiate the 7-day free trial — though you aren't billed until the trial period ends. If you don't want to be billed for a subscription, don't forget to cancel the account in time.

6. After all fields are complete, click the Start Free Access button. The Welcome to Your Fold3 Free Trial page appears, as shown in Figure 10-2.

Figure 10-2

7. Check your e-mail for the free-trial confirmation message, and follow any instructions that it contains to activate your free trial.

8. To continue using the Fold3 site, click the blue box labeled Start Searching Fold3. The web page that opens is the Search Fold3 page.

Searching Fold3 for Military Records

To search for military records at Fold3, follow these steps:

1. Go to www.fold3.com and sign in.

2. Click the Advanced Search link next to the Search button near the top of the page. The Advanced Search page appears, as shown in Figure 10-3.

Figure 10-3

3. Type the first name and last name of the person you're researching.

4. (Optional) If you know the year range, enter it into the two year fields and select a place. To refine your results, you can limit the results to material added to the Fold3 site during a particular time frame.

Every piece of information you add to the search reduces the number of results you receive. If you execute a search and receive few or no results, omit optional search criteria to try to improve your search results.

5. Click the Search button to continue. The search results page appears, as shown in Figure 10-4.

Search criteria

Number of results   Type of result

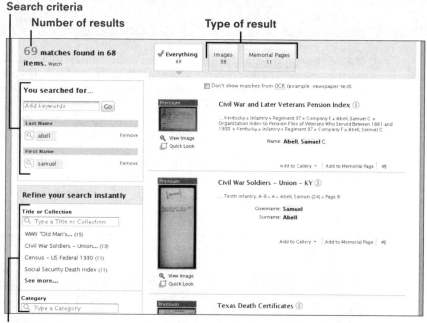

Filters

Figure 10-4

6. If you have too many results, add keywords to the Add Keywords field in the left column. If you don't have enough results, click the Remove link to delete the search term.

7. To focus your results, click a search filter in the Refine Your Search Instantly section.

   Several filters are available, including Title or Collection, Category, Last Name, First Name, Place, and Year. You can click a displayed filter or search under another filter in the Search field.

8. When you find an interesting result, click its title to see the record.

Viewing Images on Fold3

The full-featured Fold3 image viewer has several components that can help you see the best view of a scanned document. At the top of the viewing pane is a gray navigation bar. Underneath it is another bar that lets you perform specific actions on the website regarding the image. To the left of the image, a vertical bar contains tools to change the look of the image. We describe how to use each of these areas to enhance your ability to perform research on the site.

After you've opened an image in the Fold3 image viewer, shown in Figure 10-5, follow these steps to look at it in more detail:

Record set hierarchy   Search term

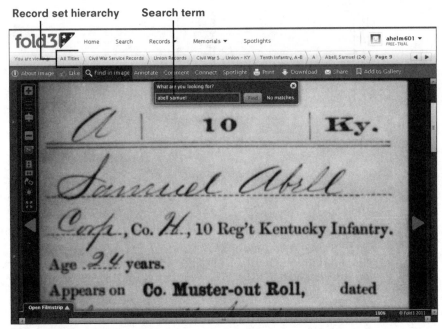

Figure 10-5

1. In the Search box near the top of the image, enter a search term to search within the image that's displayed.

   To close an onscreen element in the viewer, click the small X button in the upper-right corner of the box.

2. Use the navigation bar at the top of the image viewer to move from one portion of the record set to another. Every section (arrow) on the bar represents a level in the hierarchy. Click the level you want to view, and the browse window drops down, as shown in Figure 10-6.

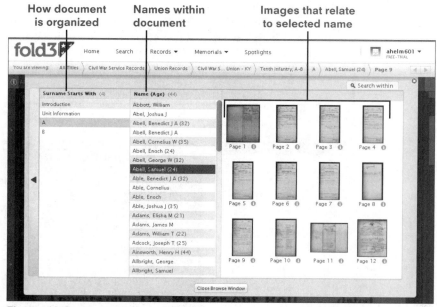

Figure 10-6

In the example, we clicked the level with the label *Abell, Samuel (24)*. The number 24 in parentheses indicates Samuel's age at the time this record was created. In Figure 10-6, you can see more than one person named Abell in the tenth Kentucky Infantry. Here's how to navigate the results:

- *Review the middle column.* This column shows the names of the individuals who have documents within this part of the collection. You can click the names of other individuals to see their documents.

- *View image thumbnails.* These small images of documents associated with the selected name are handy for navigating document collections that have lots of images. Rather than inspect every document, you can skip directly to the page you want to examine by simply clicking the image.

- *Search within links.* Click the Search Within link in the upper-right corner to uncover a search box you can use to search the images at that level. The search is particularly helpful in collections that contain lots of names or lots of text mixed with names. You can use the Search box to quickly find the person or term you're looking for.

3. When you finish exploring the browse window, click the Close Browse Window button at the bottom of the window.

4. Below the navigation bar, another bar has buttons that let you perform specific actions regarding the image, as described (from left to right) in this list:

■ *About Image:* Click the About Image button to open the Image Information pane, shown in Figure 10-7. The true value of this pane is its source information, which includes many metadata elements that you can use to record the source of the information in your genealogy database. Click the About Image button again to hide the Image Information pane.

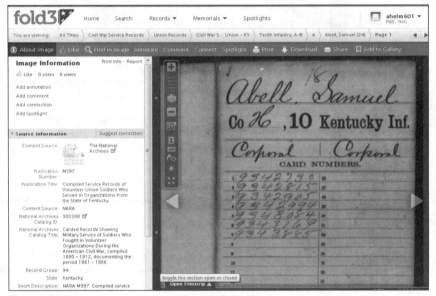

Figure 10-7

Click the Report link in the upper-right corner of the Image Information pane to tell Fold3 when something is wrong with the image or the indexed data elements. As annotations and comments are added to the image, they appear in the Image Information pane.

■ *Like:* If you like the image you're looking at, click the Like button. It's similar to the Like button in Facebook but is used only within Fold3.

■ *Find in Image:* Click this button to open the Search box (described in Step 1).

■ *Annotate:* To help index the image to make it more useful for others, click the Annotate button. Underneath the new box that appears onscreen is a box you can use to enclose text on the record in a rectangle. In the sample image, we enclosed the text *Abell, Samuel* in the rectangle, typed Samuel's name in the form on the Person tab (see Figure 10-8), and clicked the Add button.

Figure 10-8

- *Comment:* To add a comment about the image, click the Comment button and enter your text in the Comment field. Then click the Save button.
- *Connect:* You can use this button to connect an image with another image or with a particular page on Fold3.
- *Spotlight:* This feature is described in the following activity.
- *Print:* To print the image, click the Print button. In the menu that pops up, choose whether you want to print the entire image or select a portion of it.
- *Download:* To save a copy of the image, click the Download button. A pop-up box opens and lets you save the entire image or a portion of it. If you select the entire image, another box opens and asks you for a location in which to save the file. The file is saved in .jpg format. If you select a portion of an image, you must size the rectangle around the portion that you want to save and then click the Download button.
- *Share:* To share an image, click the Share button. In the dialog box that opens, choose whether to e-mail the page or post it to Facebook, Twitter, Google Bookmarks, or Delicious. Click the More link to see additional services you can post to.
- *Add to Gallery:* Click the Add to Gallery button to add a link to the image in your personal gallery. The page doesn't show that the image has been added to the gallery; however, you can view the gallery by clicking your username in the upper-right corner of the page and selecting Your Gallery. You can then link other images to this image to create a personal collection. You can even upload your own images into the gallery and link them to this image.

5. To change your view of the image onscreen, click these buttons in the toolbar to the left of the image:
   - *Zoom In/Zoom Out:* To see the image more closely (to zoom in), click the plus sign (+) on the vertical bar, next to the left side of the image, as shown in Figure 10-9. Click the minus sign (−) to zoom out.

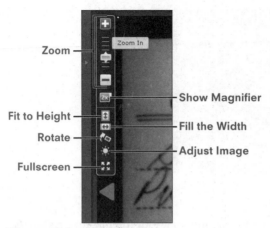

Figure 10-9

To see the full context of the information you're viewing, zoom out of the image when you first open it. Then zoom in closer to see elements more clearly. If the image is too high or too low on the screen when you zoom in and out of it, click the scroll bar on the far right side of the screen to reposition the image.

- *Show Magnifier:* When the standard zoom control doesn't let you look closely enough or it loses the context of the document, use the Show Magnifier to display a magnifying lens on the screen, as shown in Figure 10-10. You can increase the zoom by clicking the plus-sign button to the right of the magnifier.

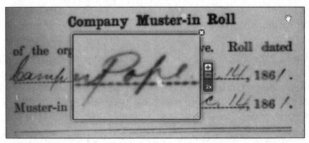

Figure 10-10

- *Fit to Height:* See the full image on the screen.
- *Fill the Width:* See the document at its full width on the screen.
- *Rotate:* Move the image 90 degrees clockwise. This button shows a curved arrow next to a tilted rectangle.

- *Adjust Image:* Change the brightness and contrast of the image. You can also invert the color of the image by selecting the Invert check box. The button looks like a shining sun.

- *Fullscreen:* View the image at its maximum size on the screen. Press the Esc key on your keyboard or click the Fullscreen button again to exit Fullscreen mode.

6. To move to another image in the collection, use one of these methods:

   - *Click the large arrow on the right side of the image to move to the next image in the collection.* When you place the cursor over the arrow, a small thumbnail of the next image appears on the screen, as shown in Figure 10-11.

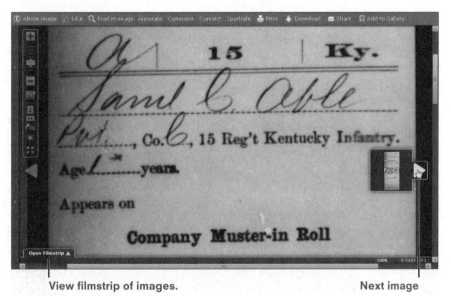

View filmstrip of images.   Next image

Figure 10-11

   - Click the Open Filmstrip link at the bottom of the page to open a window showing the few images on either side of the image you're looking at. (See Figure 10-12.) Click any image to view it. To see more images in either direction, click the arrow on either side of the filmstrip.

Current image   Portion of image currently shown

Figure 10-12

Sharing Records at Fold3

One strength of Fold3 is its sense of community. You can not only view images but also contribute your own content, in the form of *spotlights*. These articles let viewers see the context of a record or find out more about the individuals behind it.

Follow these steps to view spotlights:

1. From the Fold3 home page, click the Spotlights link at the top of the page. This step opens the Spotlights feature page, shown in Figure 10-13.

Figure 10-13

2. Scroll down the page to the Spotlights by Conflict section on the right side of the page. Click the conflict period that interests you.

You can also see links to additional featured spotlights in the Tags section on the right side of the page.

3. Click an article's link to see its full spotlight.

You can even create your own spotlights. Follow these steps:

1. Find an image to be the subject of your spotlight.
2. Click the Spotlight button on the dark gray bar along the top of the screen.
3. Move the rectangle to encompass the area to include in the spotlight, as shown in Figure 10-14.

Figure 10-14

4. Type a title, and explain why the record is interesting.
5. Click the Spotlight This button.

Reviewing Archives.com

Though the Archives.com website (launched in July 2009) is a relative newcomer to the genealogy community, it has amassed more than 1.5 billion records and historical records, such as obituaries and vital, census, and military records. Follow these steps to sign up and start searching its records:

1. Set your web browser to www.archives.com.

2. Click the orange Start 7-Day Free Trial button in the upper-right corner of the page.

3. Fill out the form with your payment information, and click the blue Begin Free Trial button. After submission, the Last Step page opens.

You can cancel your membership at any time before the 7-day free trial ends, and you won't be billed.

4. Complete the Create Your Password fields and the optional ancestor-alert information, and click the blue Create Account button. The Archives.com Welcome page opens.

The Welcome page contains general information about your surname from a dictionary of surnames. The information isn't specific to your family, so it's useful trivia about the roots of the surname.

5. Click the Historical Records Search link in the rightmost column. A new browser window or tab may open to the Members Area Search page, as shown in Figure 10-15.

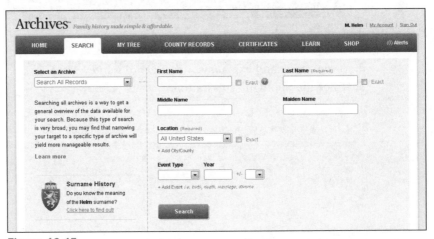

Figure 10-15

6. In the Select an Archive section, set the drop-down menu to Search All Records (the default setting). Fill in the First Name, Last Name, Middle Name, Maiden Name (if applicable), and Location fields.

You can set the First Name, Last Name, or Location fields to exact matches. If too few results are returned, disable the Exact Match check box.

7. (Optional) Fill in an event type, a year, and a date range. You can add events by clicking the Add Event link.

8. Click the blue Search button. The search results page appears, as shown in Figure 10-16. The results are arranged by record type. The same record is sometimes duplicated across record types.

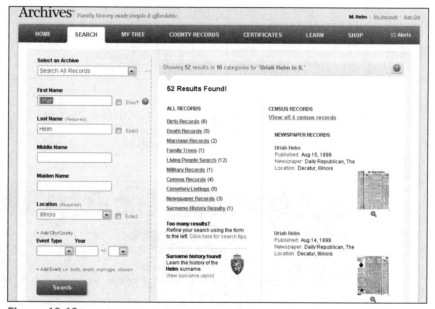

Figure 10-16

9. Click a record type to see its individual results. When we clicked the Birth Records record type, six census records were listed underneath the birth records.

10. Click the name of the person to see the full record, as shown in Figure 10-17.

Figure 10-17

11. To see an image of the record (if it's available), click the View Image button on the right side of the page. The image viewer launches and displays the digitized image, as shown in Figure 10-18.

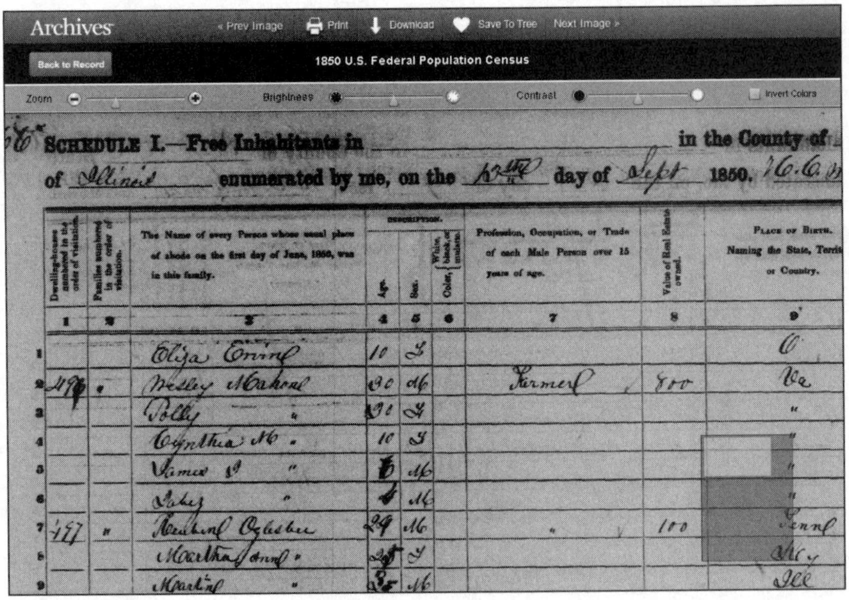

Figure 10-18

Considering census records

Though census records contain people's ages, they don't serve as primary records of birth dates and therefore aren't considered birth records. Census takers often only spoke to one person in a household about the information that was written in the census record. These individuals may or may not have known the exact ages of the individuals for whom they were providing information. You must consider the purpose of a record when you evaluate the information contained within it and its accuracy.

12. For a closer look at the image, use the zoom controls in the upper-left corner of the image viewer. You can change the brightness levels and contrast or invert colors by using the controls at the top of the viewer.

13. To print the image, click the Print button at the top of the screen. A print dialog box opens, in which you can select a printer and other options.

14. To download the image, click the Download button at the top of the screen. A file automatically downloads to your machine.

The downloaded file has no file extension. Find the file on your computer and add the .jpg extension to it so that your image viewer can open the file.

Chapter 11

Exploring Local Resources

Simply studying genealogy and family history sites isn't enough to draw a complete picture of your ancestors and their place in history. To see the whole picture, you should check out sites that specialize in local history resources, including newspapers, local history books, and your friendly local genealogical society.

tech to connect

activities

- Exploring GenealogyBank
- Finding local histories by way of Google Books
- Looking for books on WorldCat
- Paying respects at Find A Grave
- Hunting for a genealogical society

Exploring GenealogyBank

GenealogyBank specializes in obituaries, historical newspapers, and government documents. The site, owned by NewsBank, features more than 5,800 historical newspapers and a sizable government documents collection, including the American State Papers, United States Senate Journal, and United States Serial Set. You can use these resources to find references to ancestors whose names may have been mentioned in Congressional documents.

Rather than offer the standard 30-day trial period for free, GenealogyBank lets you try its site for 30 days for an introductory price that is lower than its standard subscription.

Follow these steps to use GenealogyBank to search for an ancestor:

1. Point your web browser to `www.genealogybank.com`.
2. Click the Get Access Now button on the right side of the page.
3. Fill in the First Name, Last Name, Email Address, and Phone Number fields, and click the orange Continue button.
4. Fill in the password, street address, city, zip code, country, and payment information, and click the Start Membership button to continue. The Transaction Processed page opens. Your credit card is billed at this point.
5. Click the green Continue button to return to the GenealogyBank home page.
6. Click the Advanced Search link in the upper-left corner of the page.
7. Type the last name and first name of the person you're researching. To narrow the results, type the date range of your ancestor's life span, as shown in Figure 11-1.
8. (Optional) Include a keyword with your search, such as location. You can also exclude keywords.

    Excluding keywords is useful when another person in a different location shares the same name and you want to exclude those results.

9. Click the Begin Search button. The search results page appears, as shown in Figure 11-2. Matches are grouped under general record types, such as Historical Newspapers, Historical Documents, and Social Security Death Index.
10. Select a records type link (for example, Historical Documents) from the left-most column to see details about the matches, as shown in Figure 11-3.

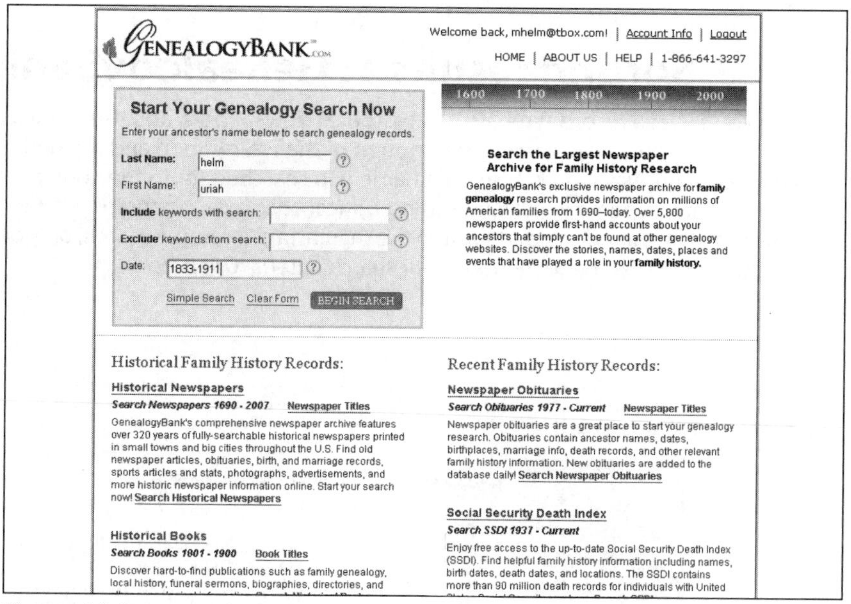

Figure 11-1

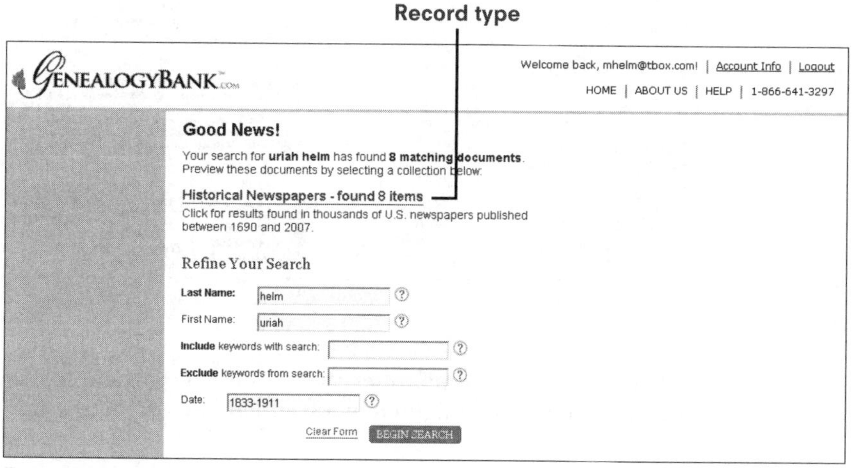

Record type

Figure 11-2

Sorting results at GenealogyBank

After you select a record type, such as Historical Newspapers, and the results are returned, you see the newspaper name, a description of the newspaper, and a thumbnail image of the article. This way, you can see the name you searched for in the context of the article. Because newspapers are searched using optical character recognition (OCR) technology, some search results aren't pertinent to the search. In our sample search, only one of the five matches on the first page mentions our search criteria, *Uriah Helm*.

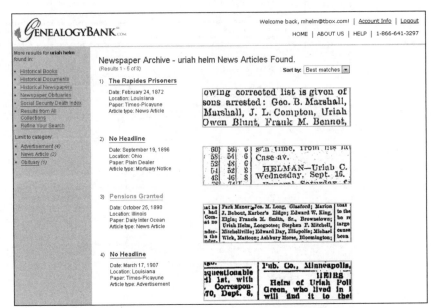

Figure 11-3

11. Click the title of a result to see the full item. For example, Figure 11-4 shows our search term highlighted in a scanned newspaper article.

Page number   PDF file   Print

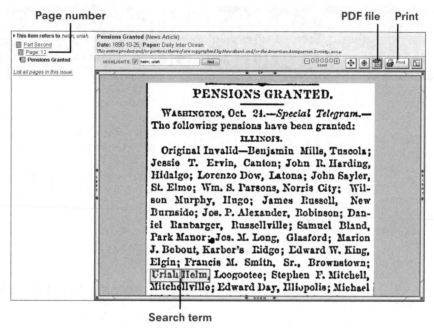

Search term

Figure 11-4

12. If you're looking at a historical newspaper, you have several options for working with it:

- *See the whole page of the newspaper.* Click the page number in the left column to see the article in the context of the full page. You might also see other, related articles nearby that you would otherwise miss. We like to save the entire page of the newspaper so that we can use its masthead as part of the source.

- *Save a copy of the newspaper image.* Click the PDF button in the upper-right corner, above the image. The image launches as an Adobe PDF document.

  Use the (free) Adobe Reader program to save the PDF document to your computer. If the Adobe PDF reader isn't installed on your computer, download it at http://get.adobe.com/reader.

- *Print the article.* Click the Print button to open your browser to another page, where you can configure the page content, page layout, paper, and size and specify whether to fit the image to the page.

Finding Local Histories by Way of Google Books

Local histories are a great way to discover what was going on in the lives of your ancestors. They often contain information about why people moved to a certain area and provide details on the daily life of people who lived in the area. Google Books digitizes a variety of books and makes them available online, either in full text, such as books in the public domain, or as previews of books that remain within copyright. In some cases, you can purchase e-books directly from the site, order print copies from a publisher, or request copies on loan from a library.

Follow these steps to search Google Books:

1. Point your web browser to books.google.com, as shown in Figure 11-5.

Figure 11-5

2. Click the Sign In link in the upper-right corner of the page, next to the gear icon.

3. If you have either a Google or Gmail account, fill in the Email and Password fields in the right column and click the Sign In button. If you don't have one of these accounts, click the Create an Account for Free link in the left column and follow the prompts to sign up.

4. In the Researching a Topic section on the left side, type a search term in the field and click the Search Books button. We typed *Fayette County Ohio history* because we want to find out more about the area. The search returned about 99,400 results.

Signing up with Google

To create a Google account, enter your current e-mail address in the first field on the Google Accounts page, choose a password, and then verify the password. Then select a location from the drop-down box. Enter your birth date and the word verification. Read the Google terms of service agreement, and then click the I Accept. Create My Account link. Google sends a confirmation message to your e-mail address. Click the URL in the message to confirm the new account and launch a web page verifying your e-mail address. To return to the Google Books page, point your web browser to `http://books.google.com`.

5. Click the title of a work to see more details.

Depending on the type of work and its access restrictions, your results may contain a few details about the book, a few preview pages, or the full-text, scanned image of a book. The search engine may not display the first page of a full-text work. We clicked the History of Fayette County link (a full-text work) to open page 634, as shown in Figure 11-6.

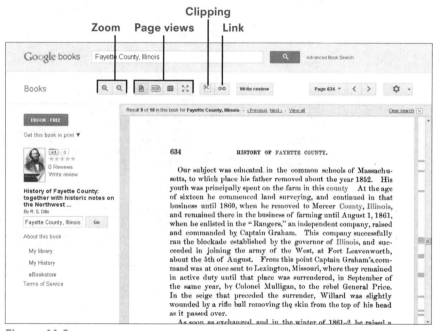

Figure 11-6

6. If you don't want search results highlighted within the work, click the Clear Search link on the right end of the yellow bar across the top of the image.

7. You can use these options to change the view of the work that's onscreen:

   - *Use the Zoom tool.* If you need a closer look at a work, click the Zoom tool (the magnifying glass with a plus sign on it). It's the first button in the row of tools across the top of the page. If you need to return to the bigger picture, look for the Zoom-out tool with the magnifying glass and the minus sign on it.

   - *Change the page view.* Change your view of the image by selecting the Single Page, Double Page, Thumbnail, or Full Screen buttons to the right of the Zoom tools.

8. To share the work, use the Clipping (scissors) or Link (chain links) tools to the right of the View tools.

When you use the Clipping tool, the cursor converts to a crosshair. Click on the screen wherever you want the clipping to begin, and drag the cursor to wherever you want the clipping to end. In the Share This Clip box that appears (see Figure 11-7), you can copy the highlighted text, copy the address as an image, or embed the URL into another page.

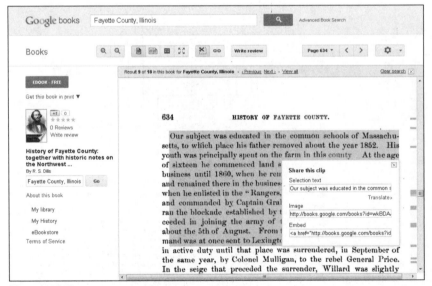

Figure 11-7

9. Depending on the type of book you're viewing, you can click the Page Number drop-down button and select another section of the book, as shown in Figure 11-8.

You can "turn" to the next or preceding page by clicking the left- or right-arrow button, respectively, to the right of the Page Number button.

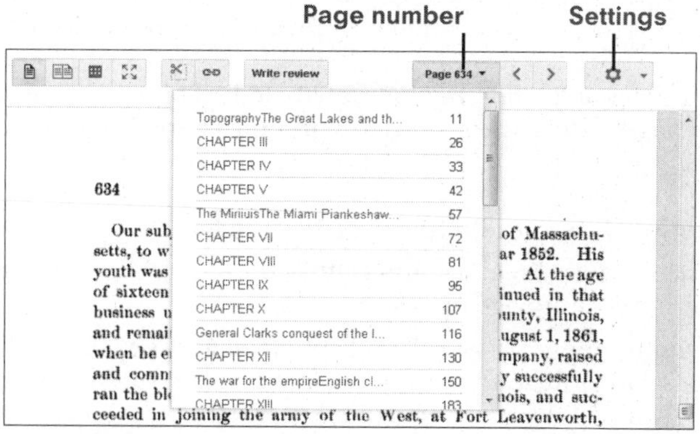

Page number   Settings

| | | | | | Write review | Page 634 ▼ | < | > | ⚙ ▼ |

TopographyThe Great Lakes and th...	11
CHAPTER III	26
CHAPTER IV	33
634	CHAPTER V	42
The MiriiuisThe Miami Piankeshaw..	57
Our sub...	CHAPTER VII	72
setts, to w	CHAPTER VIII	81
youth was	CHAPTER IX	95
of sixteen	CHAPTER X	107
business u	General Clarks conquest of the I...	116
and remai	CHAPTER XII	130
when he e	The war for the empireEnglish cl...	150
and comn	CHAPTER XIII	183
ran the bl

ceeded in joining the army of the West, at Fort Leavenworth,

Figure 11-8

10. Click the Settings drop-down button (the tiny gear) on the right end of the row of buttons to

- Save the work to your My Library area (if you have a Google account or a Gmail account)

- Download the work (if the option is available) in the form of an e-book, an Adobe PDF document, or a plain-text file

Downloaded book files can be *large*. The book in our example — a thousand page book with few illustrations — is 37 megabytes.

Looking for Books on WorldCat

The WorldCat catalog, published by Online Computer Library Center (OCLC), contains the holdings of thousands of libraries in the United States and around the world. You can search all libraries in the catalog simultaneously to find books, music, videos, and other types of digital content. The catalog is particularly helpful for finding local and family histories stored in local libraries.

After you register at WorldCat, you can create lists of books that you're interested in viewing. Follow these steps to sign up (for free) and search for books at WorldCat:

1. Set your web browser to www.worldcat.org.

2. Click the Create a Free Account button on the right side of the page. The Create an Account page opens.

3. Type a username, a password, and an e-mail address. (Don't forget to retype your password.) Read the terms of service, and select the check box indicating that you're at least 13 years old. Enter the letters you see into the Captcha box, and click the I Agree button. After creating an account, your personal account page opens, as shown in Figure 11-9.

Figure 11-9

4. Click the Advanced Search link underneath the Search field at the top of the page. The Advanced Search form opens, as shown in Figure 11-10.

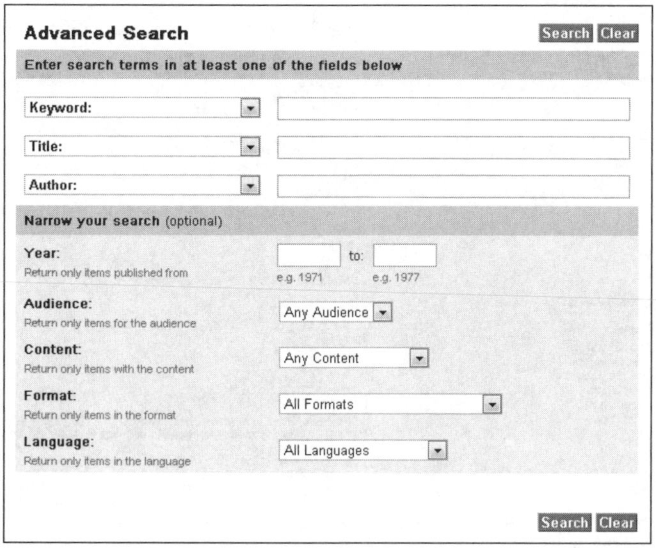

Figure 11-10

5. Type a search term, such as a family name, in the Keyword field.

6. (Optional) Select filters, such as the year, audience, content, format, or language. Click the Search button to continue. In the results page that appears, as shown in Figure 11-11, you can see the result of typing the keywords *Abell Family History.*

7. In the Format section in the first column, select the check box next to a format type to narrow your results. The results screen updates automatically.

8. Click the title to see more information about the work. We clicked the link in the third result, The Abell Family in America, as shown in Figure 11-12.

Filter results

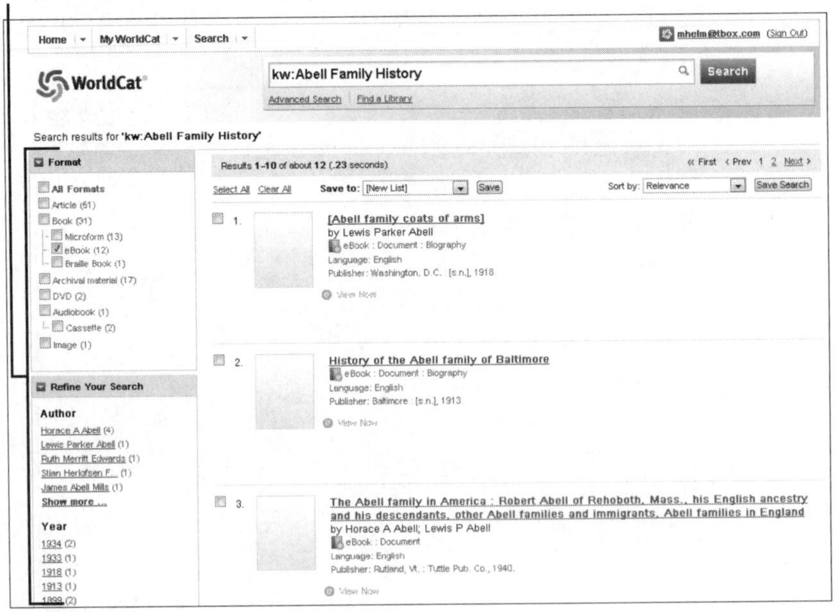

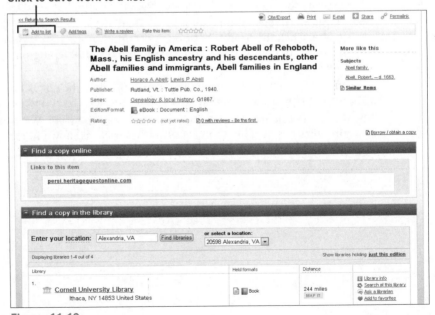

Figure 11-11

Click to save work to a list.

Figure 11-12

The entry for the search result you selected lists basic information about the work, where to find the work online, libraries that hold copies of the work, details about the work, and user-contributed reviews or tags associated with the work.

9. Click the Add to List link in the upper-left corner of the page. In the dialog box that opens (shown in Figure 11-13), choose a list — or create a new one — and click the Add to Selected List button.

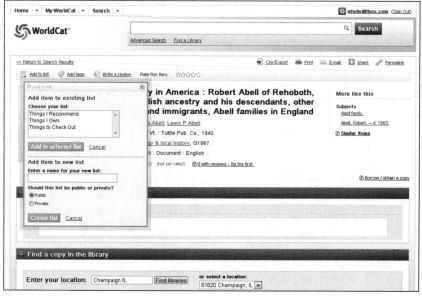

Figure 11-13

10. To see the availability of an item at a particular library, click the library name. This step begins the search in the library's own catalog system. If the catalog system's settings have changed and no results are returned, you may need to start the search again using the library's own search form.

Paying Respects at Find A Grave

The community-supported Find A Grave website documents more than 73 million grave records. More than 800,000 contributors take the time to record grave locations and take photos of cemeteries and gravestones.

Follow these steps to search for a grave location at Find A Grave:

1. Point your web browser to www.findagrave.com, as shown in Figure 11-14.

Figure 11-14

2. If you plan to contribute an entry or a photo to Find A Grave, you need to become a member. Click the Join Now link in the upper-right corner of the page. If you don't want to join, skip to Step 5.

3. Fill out the membership fields, and click the Send My Information button.

4. When you receive the message that's sent to your e-mail address, copy the activation code from the message and paste it (or type it) into the Activation Code field on the web page. Then click the Activate My Account button. The browser displays its Success message when the code is accepted.

5. In the Actions section in the upper-left corner of the page, click the Begin New Search link. If you didn't sign up in Step 2, click the link labeled Search 77 Million Grave Records. The search form opens, as shown in Figure 11-15.

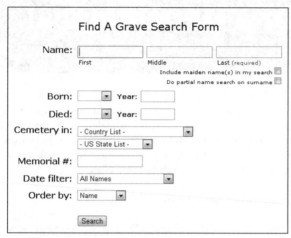

Figure 11-15

6. Type the first and last names of your ancestor. If you want, you can enter values in the Born and Died fields and use the Cemetery In drop-down list to limit the search to a particular area. Click the Search button.

7. On the Grave Search Results page, shown in Figure 11-16, click the name of the individual to see the full entry. For example, the entry for Emanuel E. Helm contains a transcription of his obituary and a picture of his gravestone. The entry also contains the location of the gravestone within the cemetery and links to his relatives' gravesites.

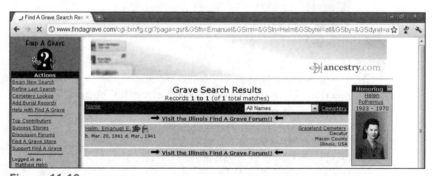

Figure 11-16

Hunting for a Genealogical Society

An easy way to find help with resources in a specific area is to contact a local genealogical society. Local societies often know of resources that speed your research, and some members might even know details about your family — especially if they lived in the locality for a long time. The Federation of Genealogical Societies, an umbrella organization for societies around the country, maintains a list of them in its Society Hall.

To locate a society, follow these steps:

1. Go to the Federation of Genealogical Societies' web page at www.fgs.org.

2. Click the Society Hall link near the bottom of the first column. The search form opens, as shown in Figure 11-17.

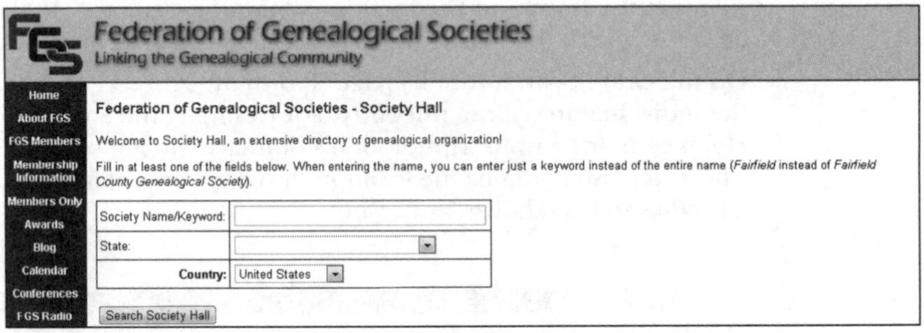

Figure 11-17

3. In the Society Name/Keyword and State fields, type the location you're interested in. Then click the Search Society Hall button. The search results page that appears is shown in Figure 11-18.

Figure 11-18

4. Click the name of the society for the contact information or, if the society has a website, click the name of the site for additional information.

Chapter 12

Connecting with Family Historians on Facebook

You're likely already a member of a social network online, such as Facebook, MySpace, or MyLife. Each of these sites is intent on putting people with similar interests or experiences in touch with each other. If you haven't considered using your social network online to further your family history research, you should know that you can. This chapter helps you explore the possibilities of using Facebook, because it's currently the largest and most popular, but keep in mind that other social networks offer similar opportunities.

activities

tech to connect

- Joining Facebook
- Creating a genealogy list
- Finding friends and adding them to your genealogy list
- Posting questions and statuses
- Communicating one-on-one
- Organizing a research group
- Uploading photos
- Participating in a family tree

Joining Facebook

The motto of the well-known Facebook social networking website says it all: "Facebook helps you connect and share with the people in your life." From its start in 2004, it now boasts some 800 million active users. If you already have a membership at Facebook, you can skip this section. If you're new to Facebook, follow these steps to join:

1. Open your favorite web browser and go to www.facebook.com.
2. In the Sign Up section on the right side of the screen (see Figure 12-1), type your first name and last name in the appropriate fields.

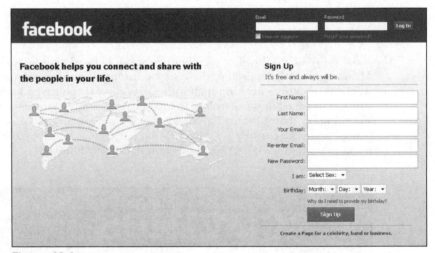

Figure 12-1

3. Type your preferred e-mail address in the Your Email and Re-enter Email fields.
4. Select a password, and type it in the New Password field.

Your password should consist of characters that you can remember but that someone else cannot easily figure out. Most public sites recommend that you create a strong password consisting of a combination of uppercase and lower-case letters, numbers, and special characters, such as percent signs (%) or exclamation points (!), but not at-signs (@) or pound signs (#).

5. Using the drop-down list, select your gender next to the words *I am*.
6. Select the month, day, and year of your birthday from the drop-down lists.

7. Click the Sign Up button. The Step 1 Find Friends page, shown in Figure 12-2, appears.

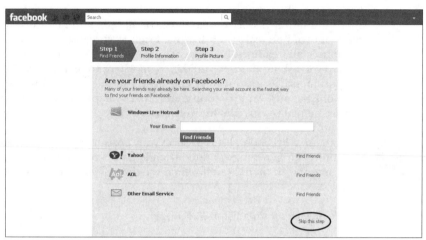

Figure 12-2

8. For now, click the Skip This Step link in the lower-right corner of the screen. You can look for friends and add them in a later activity in this chapter.

9. The Step 2 Profile Information page is next. If you want, you can complete the three fields (High School, College/University, and Employer) and then click the Save and Continue button. If you don't want to provide this information yet, click the Skip link in the lower-right corner.

10. If you want to add a photo of yourself to your profile, click the Upload a Photo link and follow the prompts from Facebook. Otherwise, click the Skip link, next to the Save and Continue button. (You can upload or change your photo later.) At this point, your Facebook profile page pops up. At the top of the page is a message saying that you need to access your e-mail account to complete the sign-up process.

11. Open your e-mail program, and open the message you received from Facebook.

12. Click the link in the e-mail message. If prompted, enter the confirmation code provided in the e-mail message. Otherwise, you should see a dialog box briefly telling you that your setup was successful and you'll return to your Facebook profile page. You're ready to start using Facebook.

After today, whenever you return to Facebook, you have to log in using the e-mail address and password that you've set up in this activity. The login fields are in the upper-right corner of the Facebook home page at www.facebook.com.

Creating a Genealogy List

Though we encourage you to use a social network for contacting and working with other family history researchers, you may experience a downside to posting about your genealogy endeavors. Friends who aren't genealogy-minded may not appreciate reading about every one of your rewarding research experiences or want you asking them for guidance on where to search next for records. If you post messages to all your friends, you run the risk of losing some of your Facebook friends. And you don't want that to happen. We recommend that you set up a genealogy-specific list in Facebook.

You can use a Facebook list to restrict your posts to a particular audience — in this case, only your genealogy-minded friends. You can choose whether to share certain content with them as well, which is helpful if you want to share photos of your ancestors.

Here's how to set up a list in Facebook:

1. Click the Home button in the upper-right corner to go to your home page.

2. Allowing the cursor to hover over the Friends section on the left side of the screen (see Figure 12-3) prompts the More link to appear. Click the More link to see the Friends page.

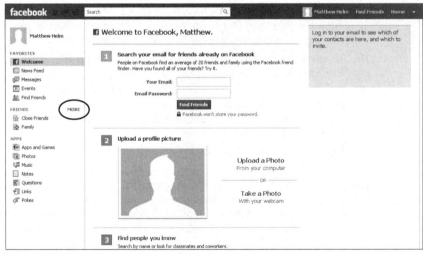

Figure 12-3

3. Click the Create List button at the top of the page. The Create New List dialog box pops up, as shown in Figure 12-4.

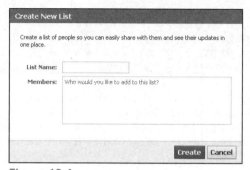

Figure 12-4

4. Type the name of your list, and then you can add friends in the Members box. Click the Create button. Your Genealogy list is created, and Facebook takes you directly to the control page for the list, as shown in Figure 12-5.

If you have a lot of friends with a common interest in a particular surname or location, you might want to use the surname or location name as the list name. Otherwise, you can name the list Genealogy, to describe your hobby or professional pursuit.

Figure 12-5

5. If you want to do so now, you can add friends directly to your Genealogy list and post a status update, pose a question to everyone on the list, or upload photos of interest to this audience.

The next three activities walk you through the steps to accomplish the tasks listed in Step 5.

Finding New Friends and Adding Them to Your Genealogy List

You need to make some Facebook friends before you can add them to the Genealogy list that you create in the preceding activity. This statement means that you likely need to look for friends and relatives who are already Facebook users. It's easy: Simply follow these steps for finding friends and adding them to your Genealogy list:

1. From your home page in Facebook or your Genealogy list page, click the Find Friends link on the left side of the screen. The Friends page appears, as shown in Figure 12-6.

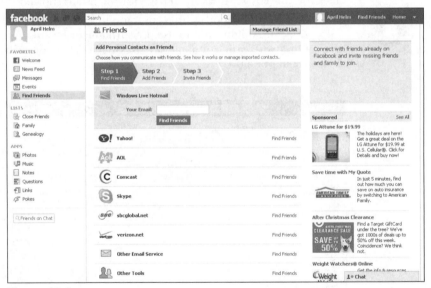

Figure 12-6

2. You can search for your friends in Facebook several ways:

   ■ If you know your friends' e-mail addresses, you can search for them by typing an address in the Your Email field. Facebook accesses your e-mail account and attempts to import email addresses from your address book. *Warning:* If your friend isn't yet a Facebook user, Facebook sends the friend an invitation from you to join.

Adding existing friends to your Genealogy list

If you forget to indicate that you want some friends to be added to your Genealogy list, you can easily add them after they accept your request. Follow these steps:

1. Go to your Facebook home page by clicking the Home button in the upper-right corner of the screen.

2. Click the Genealogy list on the left.

3. Click in the field labeled Add Friends to This List (in the middle side of the screen; refer to Figure 12-5). The Edit Genealogy dialog box appears.

4. Start typing your friend's name in the Search field.

5. Scroll the list of friends and click to select the ones you want to add to the Genealogy list.

6. Click Finish.

- If you don't want to pressure your friend to join Facebook and you simply want to see whether the friend is already a user, click the Other Tools link at the bottom of the screen (refer to Figure 12-6). When additional links expand under Other Tools, click the Find Friends, Classmates and Coworkers link. The Find Friends from Different Parts of Your Life page appears. Use the search fields to enter parameters for looking for friends. The results list on the right changes as you enter additional search parameters.

- Type a friend's full name in the Search field at the top of the page and click the Magnifying Glass icon to start the search process. The results page appears and lists people who meet your search criteria.

3. Scroll the results to see whether your friend is listed. If so, click the Add Friend button.

4. The Add Friend button changes to the Friend Request Sent button, and a pop-up menu appears, listing all your lists and groups. Select the Genealogy list for this friend, and the friend is automatically added to that list when she accepts your friendship request.

After you identify a friend or two to see the list, Facebook starts suggesting other people you might want to befriend. These recommendations are based on friends of your friends.

Posting Questions and Statuses

Collaborating with other genealogy enthusiasts on Facebook seems straight-forward: Simply post a message or profile interest indicating the family lines you're researching, and then others who might be digging into their ancestries can find you and become online friends with you.

Or you can become network friends with some of your relatives and share family stories and research findings via the site.

Though you can post a status update or a question on your main Facebook page, you should restrict genealogy-related posts to your genealogy-related list or lists so that you don't overwhelm your non-genealogy friends with research information. Here's how to restrict your posts:

1. On your home page, click the Genealogy list link on the left. (Of course, your genealogy-related list may not be named *Genealogy*, so click the appropriate list name.)

2. Type a status update in the What's on Your Mind field. When you press Enter, the status is posted, and all your friends on your Genealogy list can see it and comment on it.

3. Another way to communicate with your friends is to use the Questions function. To begin, click the Questions link in the left column in the Apps section. Then click the Question link next to the Share label near the top of the page. Type your question in the Ask Something box, and click Post. Figure 12-7 has an example.

Figure 12-7

4. Your friends can respond directly to the question after it's posted. You can update it with additional information or options, if you want. Figure 12-8 shows you what the posting looks like.

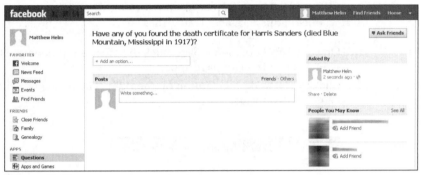

Figure 12-8

Communicating One-on-One

At some point, you may have information to share or questions that you want to ask of only one Facebook friend. Rather than post a status or question for all your Facebook friends to see (or even for only those friends on a list), you can send a one-on-one message. Follow these steps:

1. On your Facebook home page, click the Messages link on the left side of the screen. The Messages page appears.

2. Click the New Message button on the right. The dialog box shown in Figure 12-9 appears.

Figure 12-9

3. Type the name of your Friend in the To field.

4. Type your message in the Message box.

5. If you want to add an attachment, upload a photo to send, or send the message to your friend's mobile device, click the appropriate icon under the Message box.

6. Click Send.

If your friend responds to your message, you should receive an e-mail notification and see a red flag on the Notifications icon at the top of your Facebook home page. When you access the inbox of the Message section, you see the ongoing conversation between you and your friend.

Organizing a Research Group

You might find that even the Genealogy list that we tell you how to create in an earlier activity in this chapter doesn't narrow your audience enough for researching a particular ancestor or all ancestors in a specific location. Depending on how social you are, you may have hundreds of friends on your Genealogy list but only a couple dozen who are interested in exactly the same ancestor.

Or you and some friends may have a common research interest on which you want to coordinate a project. Facebook gives you the tools you need to organize a group. Follow these steps:

1. Before you create a new group, search to see whether one already exists. On your Facebook home page, click in the Search field at the top of the page, and type the term for the research group you want to form.

   For example, if April wants to find or start a group to focus research on Sanders ancestors in Tippah County, Mississippi, she would run several searches using these terms: *Sanders and Tippah County and Mississippi; Sanders and Mississippi; Sanders and Tippah County;* and *Tippah County and Mississippi.*

2. If Step 1 yields no groups that fit your needs, click the Create Group link on the left side of the screen. The Create New Group box appears. (See Figure 12-10.)

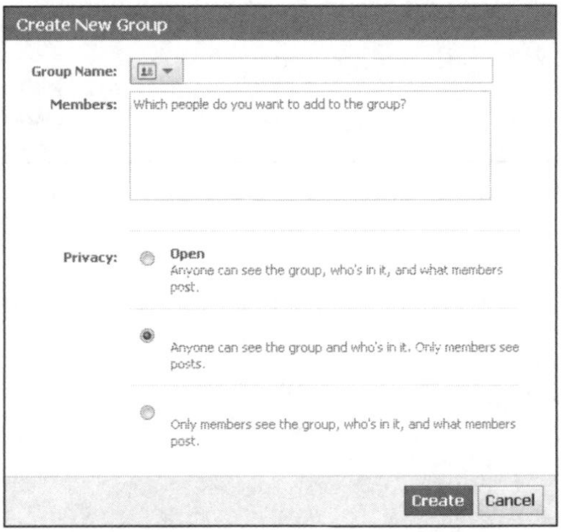

Create New Group

Group Name:

Members: Which people do you want to add to the group?

Privacy:
- Open
  Anyone can see the group, who's in it, and what members post.
- Anyone can see the group and who's in it. Only members see posts.
- Only members see the group, who's in it, and what members post.

Create Cancel

Figure 12-10

3. Using the drop-down list in the Group Name field, select an icon to represent your group. Then type the name of the group in the Group Name field.

4. Click in the Members box, and start typing the names of the Facebook friends whom you want to invite to participate in the group.

5. Select the privacy level of the group. You can choose to restrict whether others outside the group can see everything about it (the name of the group and its members and posts), only the name of the group and its members, or nothing about the group.

6. Click the Create button. This step generates your group's Facebook page, which is tied to your account. You can see our sample group page in Figure 12-11.

Figure 12-11

Uploading Photos

If you have treasured family photos or scanned copies of documents that you want to share with your Facebook friends, you can create albums and upload them directly to your Facebook account. And you can control who sees your photos — all your friends and their friends, only your friends, or only your friends who are on certain lists (such as the Genealogy list you may have created in an earlier activity in this chapter). Follow these steps to create a photo album and upload photos on Facebook:

1. On your Facebook home page, click the group name you created in the last activity in the Groups section on the left side. The Genealogy group page appears.

2. Click the Add Photo/Video link at the top of the page. The options shown in Figure 12-12 appear.

Figure 12-12

3. Click the Create Photo Album link in the rightmost box. This step opens the file manager program on your computer so that you can select the photos or images you want to upload.

4. Typically, you can highlight the filename of the photo and click the Upload or Open button. The picture you uploaded then appears in a new window.

5. Click the Album Title field, and type the name for your photo album.

   If your album will contain pictures of ancestors in a particular family line, you might use the name of the *progenitor* ancestor (earliest known ancestor in that line). Or if all the documents and photos will relate to a location, you can use the name of the location.

6. Click in the Say Something about This Album field, and type a description or an explanation of the album.

7. Click in the Where Were These Photos Taken field in the upper-right corner of the window, and type the location, if you know it.

8. Below the photo, click in the Say Something about This Photo field, and type a description of the photo.

9. If you have additional photos or images of documents to upload to this album, click the Add More Photos button at the bottom of the screen, select your photo, and type a description.

10. After you finish filling in the information for this album (see Figure 12-13), click the Post Photos button.

Figure 12-13

After your album is posted, friends on your Genealogy list can comment or post about liking the entire album or its individual images. If your photo descriptions have questions or are missing information, and any of your friends have the information, they can comment and contribute what they know or send you a private message. Likewise, if you see ancestor-related photos on a friend's Facebook pages, you can provide information to the person in the form of a comment or a private message.

If you're interested in finding out more about the ins and outs of Facebook, check out *AARP Facebook: Tech to Connect* by Marsha Collier.

Chapter 13

Testing Your DNA

When you hit the inevitable "brick wall" of being unable to find records to substantiate a person's parents or to confirm the accuracy of a paper trail, let DNA testing help. Perhaps the greatest advance in family history research in the past decade, DNA testing can be effectively used to dispel family legends or help fill in the blanks between family lines.

tech to connect

activities

- Learning about DNA testing
- Ordering a DNA testing kit
- Interpreting Y-DNA results
- Comparing mtDNA
- Finding your relatives with the Family Finder test

Learning about DNA Testing

Before you order any expensive DNA tests, read some basic information on the types of tests available and what they can tell you. You can find tutorials on the web that describe the DNA tests and their differences. The Sorenson Molecular Genealogy Foundation (SMGF), for example, has several videos. Its goal is to build the "world's foremost collection of DNA and corresponding genealogical information."

Follow these steps to see the view labeled "Introduction to Molecular Genealogy" on the SMGF site:

1. Point your web browser to www.smgf.org, as shown in Figure 13-1.

Figure 13-1

2. Click the Molecular Genealogy link in the upper-right corner of the page.
3. In the left column, click the Animations link and then the Introduction to Molecular Genealogy link.

4. Click the arrow button in the middle of the video to play it.

   The sound on your computer must be turned up in order to hear the narrated animations.

5. When the video ends, you can choose another one from the left column.

Exploring Family Tree DNA tests

Family Tree DNA, which this chapter focuses on, offers these three main types of tests:

- **Y-DNA:** Only males can take this test, because it tests the DNA that's passed directly from father to son via the Y chromosome. If you're female, a male proxy can take the test for you, such as your father, brother, uncle, or cousin.

- **mtDNA:** The DNA in mitochondria is examined. Because this type of DNA is passed from the mother to both sons and daughters, either gender can take this test.

- **Family Finder:** This test for autosomal DNA, which is inherited from both mother and father and from grandparents and great-grandparents, is used to link to relatives within the past five generations and to suggest ethnic percentages.

We use Y-DNA testing to walk you through you an example of the DNA collection process. Testing of the Y chromosome begins by swabbing inside a man's cheek with a sample collection device that usually resembles a cotton swab for cleaning ears. The swab collects cheek cells to serve as sources of the DNA. After the laboratory receives the swab, the DNA is extracted using the polymerase chain reaction (PCR) process to make thousands of copies of the DNA so that it can be analyzed. Then sequences of DNA at specific locations on the chromosome are analyzed. These sequences are *markers,* and the locations of the markers on the chromosome are *loci* (the plural of *locus*). The markers are compared to determine the testing results. (The later activity, "Interpreting Y-DNA Results," tells you more about analyzing results.)

Ordering a DNA Testing Kit

When you're ready to order a DNA testing kit, rest assured that the process is straightforward, even at the larger DNA testing facilities. DNA testing can be expensive, so be sure that you truly want to make the investment.

Choose a DNA testing company that has its own lab and that has experience with DNA in family history research. (Some companies have no testing laboratories and instead send their orders to third parties.) To ensure the best possible experience, research a company before hiring it for testing. Some examples of companies that provide genealogical services include 23andMe (https://www.23andme.com) and AncestryDNA (http://dna.ancestry.com).

We ordered a testing kit from a third company, Family Tree DNA, because it maintains its own laboratories and has provided DNA services for family historians for more than a decade. The company also provides a variety of tests and continues to expand its offerings. (See the earlier sidebar "Exploring Family Tree DNA tests.")

Follow these steps to sign up for a DNA test at Family Tree DNA:

1. Point your web browser to www.familytreedna.com, as shown in Figure 13-2.

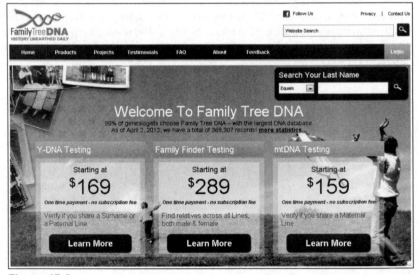

Figure 13-2

2. Click the Products button on the blue navigation bar at the top of the page.

3. In the section labeled Which Tests Are Available for You, select the radio button that matches your gender.

4. When you decide which test to take, click the Order Now button to the right of the test name, as shown in Figure 13-3. The Select a Product confirmation screen appears.

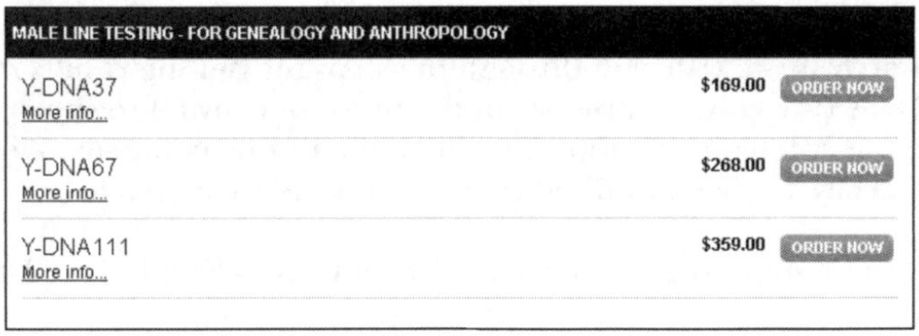

MALE LINE TESTING - FOR GENEALOGY AND ANTHROPOLOGY

Y-DNA37 $169.00   ORDER NOW
More info...

Y-DNA67 $268.00   ORDER NOW
More info...

Y-DNA111 $359.00   ORDER NOW
More info...

Figure 13-3

5. Click the Next button at the bottom of the screen.

6. Fill out the contact information for the person being tested, the shipping address, and the phone and e-mail fields. Then click the Next button.

7. Enter your payment information, and click the Next button.

8. Review your order summary, and click the Finish button. The Order Complete screen appears and lists your kit number and password.

9. When your kit arrives in the mail, follow the instructions for completing the sample and returning it to the lab. After a few weeks, you're notified that the results are ready for you to review.

Interpreting Y-DNA Results

The fun begins as soon as you receive notification that your DNA testing results are complete. Depending on which tests you ordered, the site should point you toward groups you can join to help put your results into context. And depending on who conducted your test, the site provides access to tools that can help make sense of the numbers.

In this activity, we walk you through the steps for viewing results from Family Tree DNA (the company we use in the previous activity) to show you how results can be interpreted using tools provided by a testing company. We assume that you have already been notified that your results are available.

Follow these steps to view your Y-DNA results from Family Tree DNA (FTDNA):

1. Go to the Family Tree DNA home page at www.familytreedna.com.

2. Click the Login button on the right side of the navigation menu, near the top of the page. The FTDNA login page appears.

3. Enter your kit number and password into the appropriate fields, and click the Login button. The Family Tree DNA personal page appears, as shown in Figure 13-4. The content of the page depends on the type of test you ordered.

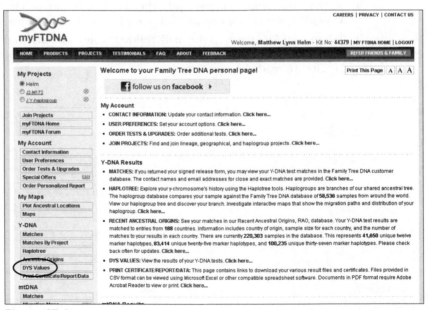

Figure 13-4

4. Click the DYS Values link in the Y-DNA section on the left side of the page.

The DYS values are presented on the web page, as shown in Figure 13-5. Every marker is given a name that usually begins with DYS — short for DNA Y-chromosome Segment. Technicians who analyze the markers look for the number of times a marker segment is repeated. These segments, known as *short tandem repeat polymorphisms* (STRPs), are represented in the FTDNA results as alleles ("uh-leels"). In the results in the figure, you can see that the number of repeats in segment DYS 393 is 12. To see whether a male is related to another male, the value of the segment is compared. The more segments that match in the samples, the more likely the two males are related.

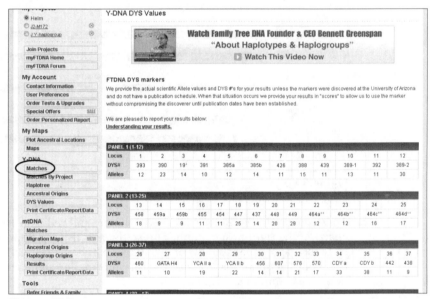

Figure 13-5

5. To compare your results with other males, click the Matches link in the Y-DNA section in the navigation column on the left.

Family Tree DNA automatically searches its databases for other individuals who match the same markers as you. The Y-DNA Matches web page lists the results of these matches, as shown in Figure 13-6. We've sanitized the results to protect participants' privacy, so you will see a name rather than the word *Private* in the first column, and you will see a live e-mail address rather than email@email.com to contact the individual. The results are arranged by the number of markers tested and the number of matching markers. If entries are designated by the characters Y37 or Y67, more than 12 markers were tested. In this instance, two individuals match at a genetic distance of 3 (the markers had at least three changes).

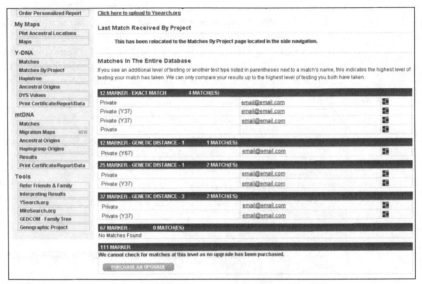

Figure 13-6

6. To understand the results, click the small blue-and-red icon (the pedigree chart) in the rightmost column. This step opens the Tip Report, which shows, by percentage, the possibility of two individuals being related within a certain number of generations. You can use this information to begin looking at potential common ancestors.

Comparing mtDNA

Mitochondrial DNA, or mtDNA, examines the DNA in mitochondria, and this DNA is passed from the mother to both sons and daughters. (For more information about mitochondria, see the sidebar "Exploring Family Tree DNA tests," earlier in this chapter.)

Follow these steps to view your mtDNA results from Family Tree DNA:

1. Follow Steps 1 through 3 in the previous activity.
2. Click the Results link in the mtDNA section.

   The mtDNA Results page, shown in Figure 13-7, lists the differences between the test sample and the Cambridge Reference Sequence (CRS). In this case, Hypervariable Region One had five differences. Hypervariable Region Two had nine differences. Together, these differences place the sample into mt Haplogroup I. A *haplogroup* is simply a grouping of several similar *haploytypes*, or sets of genetic markers for specific individuals that are used to compare the results to other individuals.

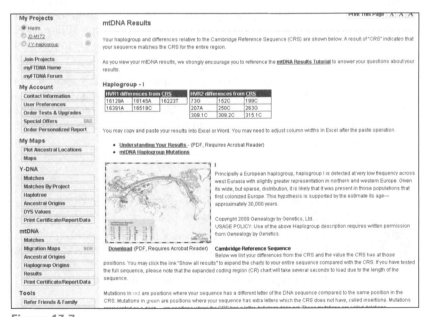

Figure 13-7

mtDNA testing 101

For testing purposes, mitochondrial DNA is divided into three regions: a coding region, Hypervariable Region One (HVR1), and Hypervariable Region Two (HVR2). Genealogical tests are usually conducted on a sequence of HVR1 or a sequence of both HVR1 and HVR2. Some testing facilities fully sequence the entire mitochondrial DNA; however, the test is expensive. The results from these sequences are compared to a sample known as the Cambridge Reference Sequence (CRS), the mitochondrial sequence of the first individual to have her mitochondrial DNA sequenced. The differences between the sample and the CRS are considered mutations for the purpose of assigning a haplogroup to the sample. If two people have the same mutations, it suggests that the individuals are related.

Because mitochondrial DNA changes (or *mutates*) slowly, its use for genealogical purposes is quite different from its use for Y chromosomes, which change at a faster rate and can link family members at closer intervals. However, mtDNA is useful for determining long-term relationships.

When two individuals have the same mutations within HVR1, the match is considered to be low-resolution. If the individuals have a low-resolution match and are classified in the same haplogroup, they have a 50 percent chance of sharing a common ancestor within the past 52 generations (about 1,300 years). If the individuals have a low-resolution match and are classified in different haplogroups, the match is considered a coincidence and the two individuals probably don't share a common ancestor within a measurable time frame. Depending on your result set, you might see a lot of low-resolution matches. To see whether a connection truly exists, test both HVR1 and HVR2.

A high-resolution match occurs whenever two individuals match exactly at both HVR1 and HVR2. Individuals having high-resolution matches are more likely to be related within a genealogically provable time frame. The individuals in a high-resolution match have about a 50 percent probability of sharing a common ancestor within the past 28 generations (about 700 years).

3. Click the Matches link in the mtDNA section in the column on the left side of the page, and review the results.

The mtDNA Matches page divides the matches into the areas HVR1, HVR1+HVR2, and Full Genome Sequence. In this case, because the results contain 104 HVR1 matches but no HVR1+HVR2 matches, the likelihood is low that this person is related to someone on the list.

Finding Your Relatives with the Family Finder Test

The Family Tree DNA Family Finder test evaluates autosomal DNA to find individuals who share a recent ancestor. Within every generation, the autosomal DNA recombines using half the DNA from each parent so that, over time, the DNA contains increasingly more changes. By comparing the amount of similar DNA in two autosomal DNA samples, testing companies can suggest how closely two people are related.

The recombination of autosomal DNA is random, and people don't necessarily inherit exactly 25 percent of their DNA from each grandparent, so an autosomal test might fail to recognize cousins. Because of the random inheritance of DNA, nothing guarantees that two cousins would inherit enough of the same DNA to appear as a match.

Follow these steps to see the results of your Family Finder test from Family Tree DNA:

1. Follow Steps 1 through 3 in the "Interpreting Y-DNA Result" activity, earlier in this chapter.
2. Click the Matches link in the Family Finder menu at the top of the page.
3. Review the results on the Matches page, shown in Figure 13-8.

The Matches page lists the name of a matching individual and the match date, relationship range, suggested relationship, shared cM, longest block, and ancestral surnames. After you identify potential matches, you can follow up with the individual to find potential ancestors.

4. Click the Population Finder link in the Family Finder section in the left column, and review the results.

The Population Finder attempts to approximate your ethnicity by comparing the autosomal DNA with profiles that have been established for ethnic groups. The interpretation of autosomal DNA is still being refined, so don't interpret the suggested ethnicity percentages as facts.

Figure 13-8

Chapter 14

Using Your iPad for Genealogy Research

Since the introduction of the iPad, the practical use of a tablet-type computer for genealogy research has held our fascination. A tablet is small enough to travel anywhere with you, yet robust enough to handle your research, data storage, navigation, and entertainment needs. You can synchronize a tablet with your computer or use it with remote-desktop applications to access your home computer directly while you're researching on the road. The tablet holds true potential for family history research.

In this chapter, we show you how to use a first-generation iPad for genealogical purposes. Though you may have a later model of the iPad or another tablet, such as a Samsung Galaxy S, a Barnes & Noble Nook, or a Sony Tablet S, the basic principles we cover in this chapter are the same. You should be able to follow the same or similar steps to perform the activities we describe. Additionally, if you have a smartphone, you may be able to use it to follow these steps, depending on the type of phone and service you have.

tech to connect

activities

- Downloading an app
- Using the Ancestry app
- Recording interviews
- Positioning yourself using MotionX
- Noting facts with Evernote
- Uploading your finds from iPad to computer

Downloading an App

The iPad comes supplied with basic applications, or *apps,* for using e-mail, text, calendars, contacts, weather sites, iTunes, the iPad applications store, and its browser. Though none of these items directly relates to genealogy research out of the box, you can use the App Store application to search for and download genealogical apps.

To download apps, you may need to know your Apple ID and password, and you have to supply a form of payment whenever you want to download a paid app.

We use the Ancestry app in this activity because it's free and it works at the Ancestry.com website (which we describe in Chapter 5). Here's how to download the Ancestry.com iPad app:

1. Fire up your iPad to see its main menu, which should look similar to the one shown in Figure 14-1. Find the App Store icon.

If the App Store icon isn't on the main menu, you may need to swipe a finger from right to left on the face of the tablet to move to the next screen to continue your search for the app.

2. Using your finger, tap the App Store icon once. This step launches the app and opens the iPhone and iPad App Store.

3. Tap in the Search field in the upper-right corner of the screen (with the Magnifying Glass icon in it), and type the word *ancestry*. A list is generated in the Results box below the Search field as you type, as shown in Figure 14-2.

4. Tap on the word *ancestry* in the Results list. The page that opens identifies all apps that fit in the selected category.

5. Browse the resulting list of apps to find the Ancestry app, from Ancestry.com. We use Ancestry in this activity because it's free and it works at the Ancestry.com website (which we describe in Chapter 5).

Notice that several other ancestry-type applications are listed. If you want to know more about any of them, simply tap its icon to have the App Store open a page with more information. Click the Search arrow in the upper-left corner to return to the previous screen.

6. Tap the Free button next to the Ancestry.com logo. This step converts the Free button to a green button labeled Install App.

7. Tap the Install App button.

8. If a pop-up message asks for your Apple ID and password, type the password in the appropriate field and click OK. As the app starts downloading, the App Store minimizes, and the iPad returns to the main menu and shows you its progress on a bar underneath the icon for your new app. After the download is complete, you're ready to start using the Ancestry app.

Figure 14-1

Figure 14-2

Using the Ancestry App

The Ancestry app from Ancestry.com is a handy way to create your family tree and add to it as you research. You can build a new tree in the app or link to a tree you've already started on Ancestry.com, as described in Chapter 2. The data is laid out like a *pedigree chart,* which shows a primary person and lines representing relationships to the person's parents and lines connecting the parents to their parents, and so on, so it's rather intuitive. And its Ancestry Hints and Shaky Leaves hints assist you with your research by recommending places to look for additional information about ancestors.

Follow these steps to see how to use the Ancestry app to add information to your family tree:

1. Open your iPad and find the Ancestry app icon. You can see in Figure 14-3 what the icon looks like.

Figure 14-3

2. Using your finger, tap the Ancestry app once. The first task that the app asks you to complete is to sign up for an Ancestry account or to sign in, if you already have an account.
3. If you already have an Ancestry account (refer to Chapter 5), you can sign in. Tap the Sign In button and provide your username and password, followed by tapping the Sign In button again. If you don't have an Ancestry account, tap the Sign Up Now button and follow the prompts from Ancestry to create one.
4. If you already have begun creating a family tree at Ancestry.com, the app presents a list of available family trees. Tap the family tree you want to update.

    If you want to start a new tree, tap the plus sign (+) in the upper-right corner of the box. In the appropriate fields, type the first name, last name, and gender of the person who should be the starting point for this family tree.
5. Starting with the person who is the focal point of your tree, tap the Add New Life Event button to open the Add Event dialog box.

6. Fill in the details of the event, as follows:

- Select the event type by tapping the Type field and then scrolling the list and tapping the appropriate choice.
- Tap the Date field to add the date of the event. Use the rolling calendar at the bottom of the Event Date dialog box to select the date, as shown in Figure 14-4.

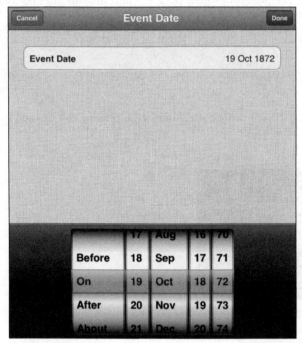

Figure 14-4

- If you know the location of the event, tap the Location field to open the Event Location form. Type the name of the location in the Search field. As you type, the app generates a Results list. Tap the appropriate result.
- If you want to add a description of the event, tap in the Description field. In this free-form text field, you can simply type whatever you want and then tap Done.

7. Repeat Step 6 as necessary to add the known life events of your focal person and help build the data in your family tree. When you add a marriage event, you have the opportunity to add the person's spouse. Figure 14-5 shows you what our sample tree looks like after adding basic life events for John Sanders.

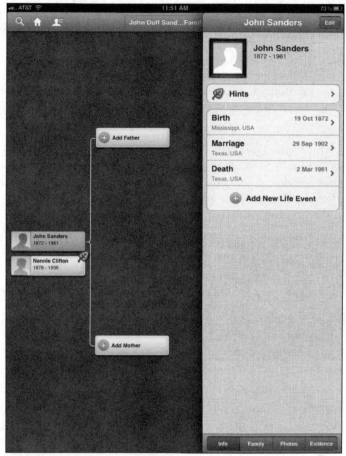

Figure 14-5

8. After you have entered one or more life events for the main person in your tree, tap the box highlighting one of that person's parents. The app walks you through the same steps to add the parent's information and life events. For every person you add, the app creates two new boxes — one for each parent.

9. To return to the overall Family Tree view, you can tap the Home icon at the top of the app. Anytime you want to return to the editing pane, you can tap the name of the ancestor for whom you want to enter facts from the family tree or tap the icon showing three horizontal lines next to a person's head, in the upper-left corner of the screen.

Press the left-pointing arrow at the top of the app with an ancestor's name on it to move backward through the tree one generation at a time, or sweep your finger across the screen to move more quickly through the family tree.

Recording Interviews

Depending on which generation of iPad you have, you may be able to record interviews with relatives on video for your genealogical purposes. If you have a first-generation iPad, you can record the audio of your interviews even though you cannot record them on video. Follow these steps:

1. Open your iPad, and follow the steps in the first activity in this chapter to download the QuickVoice Recorder app. It's free at the App Store, and you can find it by searching for the phrase *voice recorder* or *QuickVoice Recorder*.

2. After you download QuickVoice Recorder, find it on your iPad's main menu (shown in Figure 14-6) and tap it once to open it.

QuickVoice

Figure 14-6

3. Tap the Title button at the bottom of the screen, and add a title for your interview, such as the one shown in Figure 14-7. Tap the Save button.

4. Tap the Record button to start recording.

tech tip

Remember to state an introduction when you first start recording so that you can easily determine who was interviewed and where and when the interview took place. The introduction is handy in case the title is ever overwritten or you have multiple relatives with the same name or you decide to forward the recording to another person or device and the title doesn't transfer with the recording. You can start with simple text, such as "This is [your name] interviewing [relative's name and how they relate to you, such as grandmother, cousin, uncle] in [name of town] on [date]."

5. To pause the recording, tap the Pause button. To stop recording altogether, tap the Stop button.

6. To play back the interview, highlight the interview you want to hear in the list and tap the Play button.

7. If you want to forward the voice recording to an e-mail address, tap the folder icon with the arrow extending from it at the bottom of the screen. Then

select Email Recording, shown in Figure 14-8, and follow the prompts to create and send an e-mail message.

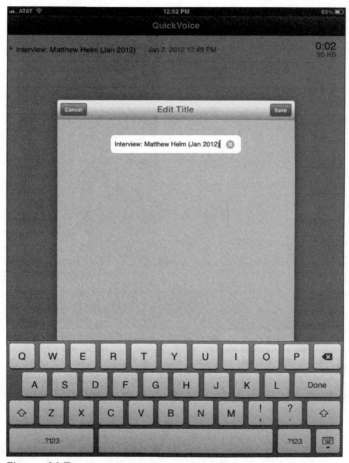

Figure 14-7

8. If you need to delete the recording for any reason, highlight it in the list and tap the Garbage Can icon at the bottom of the screen.

9. When you finish using the QuickVoice Recorder app, press the iPad Home button (in the lower-front area of the iPad) to close the app.

Figure 14-8

Remember that even though you've closed an app, it remains running in the background for multitasking, so you need to double-click the iPad Home button and exit the app if you're truly finished using it.

Positioning Yourself Using MotionX

When you're traveling for genealogical research, sometimes it's helpful to use a global positioning system, or *GPS*.

We find GPS particularly useful for these tasks:

- Finding cemeteries and gravestones
- Logging latitude and longitude for locations where our ancestors had significant events

Many mobile devices, including tablets, use GPS. On the iPad, there are several thousands of apps that use GPS. We use the MotionX app, because it's designed for using terrain maps in an off-road setting — perfect for conducting genealogy research in the field. The catch is that MotionX isn't free; to download and use it, you have to pay. Other GPS apps are available, and a couple are free, so if you prefer to try a free one first, you may need to modify the following steps slightly. You can still complete this activity by substituting the free app for MotionX. Follow these steps:

1. Open your iPad, and follow the steps in the first activity in this chapter to download the MotionX app. You can find it by searching for *MotionX*. Because you have to buy this app, your Apple ID and password are required.

2. After you download MotionX, find it on your iPad's main menu, shown in Figure 14-9, and tap it once to open it.

Figure 14-9

3. When you see the "Use of MotionX GPS" notice, read it, and tap the Agree button if you agree to its terms of use.

4. If you receive an important note from MotionX, read it and tap the Done button. This step opens the map and pinpoints your current location. If you're using the GPS to determine the latitude and longitude of a location and you're standing at that location, you can look in the upper-right corner of the map to see the current latitude and longitude. Figure 14-10 shows the map with latitude and longitude.

Figure 14-10

5. Tap the Menu button to see the activities that you can set MotionX to do for you, including working as a compass, tracking waypoints on your journey, and marking tracks on the map (like breadcrumbs).

6. From Map view, tap the Search button (the Magnifying Glass icon). This step opens the Search wheel, shown in Figure 14-11.

Figure 14-11

7. Tap the Coordinates section of the Search wheel. It's labeled Lat Lon.

8. Tap the Lat button at the top of the screen, and enter the latitudinal coordinates by using the rolling bars to select values (for example, **38 55.58 N**).

9. Tap the Lon button, and enter the longitudinal coordinates by using the rolling bars to select values (for example, **088 54.18 W**). Figure 14-12 shows you what the screen should look like.

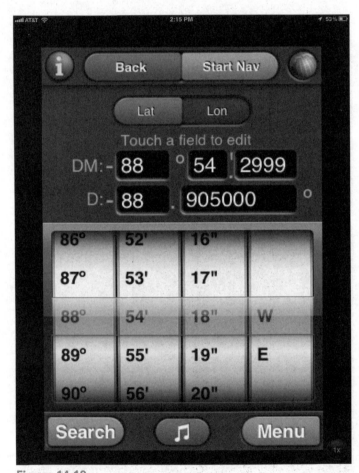

Figure 14-12

10. Tap the Start Nav button. MotionX plots the path from your current location to the coordinates you have entered as green dots.

Notice that the path doesn't necessarily follow roads. That's because MotionX is calculating the direct path between two sets of coordinates, not mapping from one location to another.

11. When you finish using the MotionX app, press the iPad Home button (in the lower-front area of the iPad) to close the app.

Noting Facts with Evernote

Evernote, the free — and useful — productivity app for the iPad, helps you organize your ideas and gives you a place to write free-form notes. You can use the app to record and store notes, create to-do lists, capture photos, and record audio files (which are helpful as vocal reminders).

- Record formal notes in meetings or research
- Create reminder notes
- Collect images of documents and articles

To begin exploring the many uses of Evernote, follow these steps:

1. Open your iPad, and follow the steps in the first activity in this chapter to download the Evernote app. You can find it by searching for *Evernote*. You may be asked to provide your Apple ID and password.

2. After you download Evernote, find it on your iPad's main menu, shown in Figure 14-13, and tap the app once to open it. If you don't have an existing Evernote account, click the Create an Account button and follow the instructions to continue.

Figure 14-13

When you open Evernote, all your existing files appear in the default All Notes view, with all notes in chronological order. You may have to scroll down to see all of them.

3. To change the view, tap an option along the top of the screen:
    - **All Notes:** The default view
    - **Notebooks:** Files sorted by category or similar topic
    - **Shared:** Files you share with others
    - **Tags:** Files in which you've tagged other people
    - **More:** Files sorted by place or search

    Figure 14-14 shows you what Evernote looks like when you first open it.

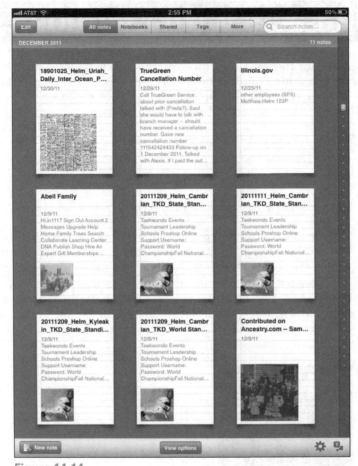

Figure 14-14

4. To review or edit an existing document, simply tap its filename to open it. You can tap the icons along the bottom of the screen to initiate an action:

  ▪ **Round arrow:** Refresh the document.

  ▪ **Trash can:** Delete the document.

  ▪ **File with arrow:** Send or forward the document to a Facebook, Twitter, or e-mail account or print it.

  ▪ **Pencil:** Edit the text portion of a note.

  ▪ **Magnifying glass:** Search the text for specific words.

5. To create a new note file, tap the New Note button in the lower-left corner of the screen.

6. In the Title field, type a title for your notes. When you research a particular ancestor, we recommend that your title include these elements:
   - The ancestor's name
   - The type of event you're researching, such as birth, job, or death
   - The research location, such as the name of the library and town
   - The date (though Evernote records the date on the file for you)

7. Though the Notebook identifier may autopopulate based on your Evernote settings, you can change the identifier by tapping the field and selecting from the Notebooks list.

8. The Tags field default setting is blank. To remind yourself that another person is involved with that particular task, add the person's name to the Tag field.

9. In the large, white area underneath the Tags row, start typing whatever you want in a free-form note.

10. When you finish taking notes, tap the Save button in the upper-right corner of the screen.

11. When you finish using the Evernote app, press the iPad Home button (in the lower-front area of the iPad) to close the app.

Uploading Your Finds from iPad to Computer

Depending on which generation of iPad you have, you can move the following types of data from the tablet to your computer in a variety of ways, if you want:

- **Photos, audio or video recordings, and notes:** You can typically e-mail them to yourself.
- **Files from apps that are associated with more traditional versions of software that are resident on your computer:** You can typically upload them by connecting your iPad to your computer.

Here's how to connect your iPad directly to your computer:

1. Using the connector cord that comes supplied with your iPad, insert the iPad end of the cord into the iPad, and insert the USB end into the USB port on your computer. This action should prompt iTunes and other applications to open automatically, depending on which applications are installed on the iPad.

2. If prompted to upload new data, files, or photos, follow the prompts to complete the process.

   Voilà! Your computer and iPad begin communicating, and your computer should begin prompting you about which files to synchronize.

Index

G

S

Z

zooming records
  Ancestry.com, 69
  Fold3, 145–146
  Google Books, 161
  HistoryGeo.com, 132–133